KU-744-923

Landscapes of
WESTERN
CRETE

a countryside guide
Third edition

Jonnie Godfrey and Elizabeth Karslake

SUNFLOWER
BOOKS

Third edition 1997
Sunflower Books™
12 Kendrick Mews
London SW7 3HG, UK

ISBN 1-85691-095-4

*Right: church at Stalos
(Walk 1)*

Important note to the reader

We have tried to ensure that the descriptions and maps in this book are
error-free at press date. The book will be updated, where necessary,
whenever future printings permit. It will be very helpful for us to receive
your comments (sent in care of the publishers, please) for the updating
of future printings.

We also rely on those who use this book — especially walkers —
to take along a good supply of common sense when they explore.
Conditions change fairly rapidly on Crete, and **storm damage or bull-
dozing may make a route unsafe at any time**. If the route is not as we
outline it here, and your way ahead is not secure, return to the point of
departure. **Never attempt to complete a tour or walk under hazardous
conditions!** Please read carefully the notes on pages 37 to 43, as well
as the introductory comments at the beginning of each tour and walk
(regarding road conditions, equipment, grade, distances and time, etc).
Explore **safely**, while at the same time respecting the beauty of the
countryside.

Cover: descent to Loutro (Walk 23)
Title page: the White Mountains (Levka Ori)

Photograph page 4: Jeremy Hosking; photographs pages 118-119 and
  131: Tanya Tsikas; all other photographs: Elizabeth Karslake
Maps and plans: Pat and John Underwood
A CIP catalogue record for this book is available from the British Library.
Printed and bound in the UK: KPC Group, Ashford, Kent

10 9 8 7 6 5 4 3 2 1

Contents

4 Landscapes of Western Crete

THE WALKS

Jonnie (left) and Elizabeth on the path to Elafonisi (Walk 18)

❀ Preface

Mountains rearing straight up from the sea, deep wooded gorges, ravines and valleys — and yet more glorious mountains, standing proud and acting as a magnet to the eye and the imagination — that's western Crete, or real Crete, as some would say. Its strong, dramatic scenery and colours create sweeping landscapes of harsh but beautiful countryside — countryside that has been the backdrop for heroic deeds, ancient civilisations and constant intrigue for thousands of years, and the home of obdurate, tough people — made so by their labours on the land and their experiences.

Getting to know western Crete takes time, and it is still a minority who explore beyond the obvious. We hope we will lead you straight to the heart of the matter with this book, whether you are a first- or second-time visitor unsure about how best to get to know the island or, indeed, if you are someone who doesn't need convincing but would like a reliable, thorough and different guide. We encourage you to explore to the full. We won't need to inspire you; one look at western Crete will do that.

Landscapes of Western Crete, in the same tried and tested format as the other titles in the series, takes you well off the beaten track, while at the same time describing in full the most popular touring routes and excursions. This Third edition, as well as being a thorough update with new maps, includes many new walks based on Rethimnon.

Everyone has heard of the Samaria Gorge, and rightly so. But frankly, anyone who contemplates walking the gorge — a long and by no means unchallenging expedition — could accomplish a number of other walks in this book and gain a great amount of pleasure in alternative landscapes. What's more, walking just about anywhere else in western Crete will give the added bonus of solitude and perhaps an even greater feeling for the island and its people, who vary both in style and character from region to region.

Acknowledging the fact that western Crete attracts a number of visitors who choose to have more than one base, or who don't feel obliged to return to their villa, hotel or apartment every night, we have described walks that can be linked and which cover a large expanse of the western end of the island. Western Crete lends itself to this arrangement very well. These walks start above the Samaria Gorge, in the awe-inspiring White Mountains — Levka Ori (even when they're not snow-capped, their peaks are a striking white, hence their name).

We have been asked, often, if and how western and eastern Crete differ from one another. In fact we naturally made the comparison ourselves in the course of compiling this second guide, having previously written Landscapes of Eastern Crete. The west is even more mountainous and less developed than the east; the geography is such that walks tend to be longer and the terrain, on the whole, rougher in the west. And the people of western Crete are somewhat more reserved than their counterparts in the east. Western Crete has its own captivating and entrancing character. You simply need to immerse yourself in the countryside to find out.

— JONNIE GODFREY

Acknowledgements

We would like to express our gratitude to the following people:

Antonis Pavlakis, of Pavlakis Beach Apartments at Stalos, whose generosity and willingness made all things possible;

Tanya and Themos Tsikas, for unstintingly checking walks and details — and for their enthusiasm and professionalism;

Lynne and Bob Tait and John Channon, for their valuable contributions, suggestions and help;

Aptera Travel, Josef Schwemberger, Yiannis Yiakoumakis, Chrys and Cres Crescini, the Tsotsolakis and Tsontos families — for Cretan hospitality, which includes support, encouragement, sustenance, fetching, carrying and firm friendship;

Hermione Elliott, B Geipel, Jeremy Hosking and Nicholas Janni — for their individual, very much appreciated contributions.

Background reading

John Bowman: *The Travellers' Guide: Crete* (Jonathan Cape, 1974)
Pat Cameron: *The Blue Guide: Crete* (A & C Black, 1995)
David MacNeil Doren: *The Winds of Crete* (John Murray, 1974)
John Fisher and Geoff Garvey: *The Rough Guide to Crete* (Rough Guides, 1996)
Adam Hopkins: *Crete: Past, Present & Peoples* (Faber, 1977)
Nikos Kazantzakis: *Zorba the Greek* (Faber, 1996)
W Stanley Moss: *Illmet by Moonlight* (Buchan and Enwright, 1994)
Oleg Polunin: *Flowers of the Mediterranean* (Chatto, 1996)

❀ Getting about

Hiring a car is certainly the best way to get to know Crete. There's no denying that it's quite costly, but we hope that by giving you some good itineraries, you will be able to make the most of the island — and your car. Many of the tours we suggest will take you past the starting- and/or end-points of several walks. In fact, seeing the countryside from a car will encourage you, we hope, to go off the beaten track and into the hills with us, on foot.

Taxis are an alternative way to tour and, if shared, can be a reasonably-priced way to travel. Do agree a fare before you set out, if it's going to be an unmetered journey. Your holiday company's agent or representative will help you to find a driver who speaks English and who will be happy and proud to show off his island.

Organised excursions are good value; coaches eat up the kilometres while you sit back and watch it all go by.

One of the best ways of getting about is by **local bus**. Once you've done it for the first time, you'll realise it's economical, reliable and entertaining. You'll whizz along the highways and bumble through villages with a bus-eye view over the countryside. Use the local bus network to explore western Crete economically. The plans on the following pages show you where the bus stations are in Hania and Rethimnon. Timetables for buses covering the western half of the island are on pages 133-134. *Note: Please be sure to pick up a current bus timetable* at the station before you plan any excursions: the frequency of services changes with the seasons. For complete assurance, verify the times in advance by asking. If you are lucky, the officials at Hania bus station (where, incidentally, there is a left luggage facility) will tell you the number of the bus you want, but they won't know it themselves much in advance of departure. Arrive in good time, as buses leave promptly and sometimes even *earlier* than scheduled, particularly those that depart at the crack of dawn. Most tickets are bought at the depot before boarding, including those to Samaria (the 'Omalos' bus). If you *do* buy tickets on the bus, don't be confused if you get three per person for just one trip — they add up to the total. You can flag down buses en route, but they don't always stop. *Always* put your hand out, even at a bus stop.

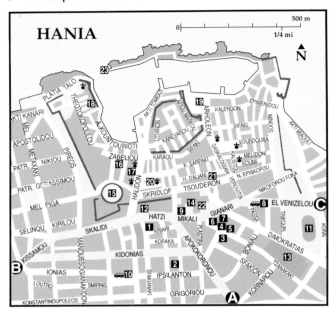

HANIA — KEY

1 Tourist information bureau
2 Tourist police
3 Olympic Airways terminal and Greek Alpine Club (EOS)
4 Post office
5 Telephone and telegraph (OTE)
6 National Bank of Greece
7 Bank of Greece
8 🚌 for Akrotiri
9 🚌 for Akrotiri, Iraklion, Souda, Mournies and town routes
10 🚌 for Alikianos, Aptera (beach), Hora Sfakion, Kalamaki,
   Kandanos, Kastelli, Lakki, Meskla, Omalos (Samaria), Paleohora,
   Platanias (beach), Platanos, Rethimnon, Sougia, Xiloskala
   (Samaria)
11 Stadium
12 Ionian and Popular Bank
13 Public gardens and zoo
14 Market
15 Shivao bastion
16 Venetian loggia
17 Archaeological museum
18 Maritime museum (Firka tower)
19 Customs
20 Cathedral
21 Minaret
22 Hospital
23 Lighthouse

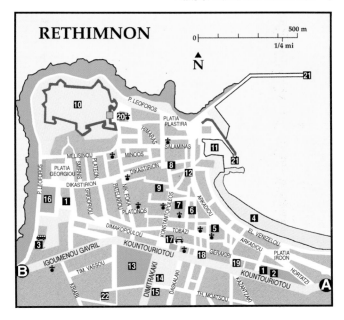

RETHIMNON — KEY
1 Tourist information bureau (two locations)
2 Post office
3 🚌 Bus station
4 Public beach
5 Youth hostel
6 Greek Commercial Bank
7 National Bank of Greece
8 Arimondi fountain
9 Nerantzes fountain
10 Venetian fortress
11 Venetian harbour
12 Museum (Venetian loggia)
13 Public gardens
14 Funfair
15 Bank of Greece
16 Stadium
17 🚕 Taxi rank
18 Telephone and telegraph (OTE)
19 Town hall
20 Archaeological museum
21 Lighthouse
22 Hospital

Picnicking

Picnicking on Crete is not an organised affair. There aren't any specially-provided sites; it's very much a case of pick your own olive tree and toss for the best view. So we can't tell you where there are tables and benches for picnickers; there aren't any. But following is a selection of some good places to throw down a towel or a rug (it's unlikely to be wet, but it might well be prickly) and revel in the countryside. Don't forget the corkscrew ...

There are 17 picnic suggestions. All have been chosen for ease of access and none involves too much climbing or lugging of provisions. All the information you need to get to these picnic places is given on the following pages, where *picnic numbers correspond to walk numbers*. (The three picnic suggestions on page 12, prefixed 'CT', are specifically linked to the corresponding car tours.) You can quickly find the general location on the island by looking at the pull-out touring map, where the area of each walk is outlined in white.

We include transport details for those travelling by car or bus, and how long you'll have to walk. Beside the picnic title you'll find a map reference: the location of the picnic spot is shown on this *walking* map by the symbol **P**, while 🚌 and 🚗 symbols indicate the nearest bus and car access. Some of the picnic settings are illustrated.

This delightful old bridge over the Platys River in the Amari Valley (Car tour 8) is the lovely setting for Picnic CT8. Psiloritis rises in the background. Walks 28 and 29 are set in this area, which sheltered many Resistance fighters during World War II.

If you're travelling to your picnic by bus, be sure to arm yourself with an up-to-date bus timetable from the nearest bus station. **If you are travelling by car**, be extra vigilant off the main roads; children and animals are often in the village streets. Without damaging plants, do park *well off* the road; *never* block a road or track.

All picnickers should read the country code on page 13 and go quietly in the countryside.

1 AGIA LAKE (map page 45; photograph page 46)

🚗 by car: up to 5min on foot. Drive from Agia towards Kirtomados and park on the track to the lake, just beyond a bridge with iron railings.
🚌 by bus: about 20min on foot. Follow the Short walk on page 44.

2 VIEWS FROM THERISO (map pages 48-49)

🚗 by car: about 10min on foot. Use the touring map to drive to Theriso, south of Hania, in the foothills of the White Mountains (you are also near Theriso if you follow Car tour 3). At Theriso use the notes on page 47 to drive along the track that Walk 2 follows — as far as the bridge (the 10min-point in the walk). Park here, well off the track, and then follow the path referred to in the walking notes for some 5-15 minutes.
🚌 by bus: about 20min on foot. Follow Walk 2, page 47, climbing the path above the watercourse as far as you like.

3a VIEWS FROM KATOHORI (map pages 54-55)

🚗 by car: under 5min on foot. Follow Car tour 5. Coming downhill into Katohori, on a big U-bend to the right (where there is a miniature concrete church), take the concrete track to the left. Continue to the small square before the bridge, and park. Then follow Walk 3, page 50.
🚌 by bus: about 15min on foot. Follow Walk 3, page 50.

3b GORGE NEAR KATOHORI (map page 54-55, photograph page 51)

🚗 by car: about 15min on foot. Park as for Picnic 3a above, then follow Walk 3 (page 50), to picnic in the waymarked gorge.
🚌 by bus: about 30min on foot. Follow Walk 3, page 50.

4 KAMBI (map pages 54-55)

🚗 by car: under 10min on foot. Follow Car tour 5, and park in Kambi. Then follow Walk 4 (page 52).
🚌 by bus: under 10min on foot. Follow Walk 4 (page 52).

6 KOURNAS LAKE (map pages 58-59)

🚗 by car: up to 10min on foot. Follow notes for Car tour 6 on page 32. Having passed the lake at Kournas, park near the bridge.
🚌 by bus: about 45min on foot. Take a bus to Georgioupoli (Timetables 1, 2); then follow Walk 6 in reverse.

8a VIEWS OVER RETHIMNON (map pages 64-65)
8b PICNIC IN THE PINES (map pages 64-65)

🚗 by car: up to 5min on foot. Car tours 6, 7, and 8 take you to Rethimnon. From Rethimnon drive to the chapel of Profitis Ilias above the town. To get there, head south uphill on Theotokopoulou Street (at the eastern side of the town; this is the road to Roussospiti). Turn right into the track to the church and park. Picnic here, or in the pines five minutes above the chapel (notes page 67).
🚌 by bus: about 20-25min on foot. Follow Walk 8, page 66.

Here's a welcome opening in the (generally steep and narrow) Imbros Gorge — the setting for Picnic 25.

13 POLIRINIA (map pages 82-83, photograph page 79)

🚗 by car: about 20-25min on foot. Follow Car tour 1 and take the detour to Polirinia (page 17, paragraph 4). Park near the taverna at the end of the road and follow notes for Walk 13 (page 78), but in reverse.

🚌 by bus: about 20-25min on foot. Ask in Kastelli about buses to Polirinia. Then follow the notes for Walk 13 (page 78), but in reverse.

14 KATSOMATADOS (map pages 82-83, photograph page 81)

🚗 by car: under 10min on foot. Follow Car tour 1 to Katsomatados, 3km south of Topolia (page 19). Then use notes on page 80 (Walk 14) to picnic near the start of the walk.

🚌 by bus: under 10min on foot. Follow Walk 14, page 80.

17 SOUGIA (map pages 88-89, photograph page 21)

🚗 by car: about 10-15min on foot. Follow Car tour 3 and park in Sougia, then use the notes for Walk 17 on page 88.

🚌 by bus: about 10-15min on foot. Follow Walk 17, page 88.

25 IMBROS GORGE (map pages 114-115, photograph above)

🚗 by car: about 20min on foot. Follow Car tour 6 to Imbros and park in the village. Then use notes on page 111 (Walk 25).

🚌 by bus: about 20min on foot. Use notes page 111 (Walk 25).

27 MEGALOPOTAMOS RIVER (map page 117)

🚗 by car: about 30min on foot. Follow Car tour 6 to Asomatos and park in the village. Then use notes on pages 117-118 (Walk 27).

🚌 by bus: about 30min on foot. Use notes pages 117-118 (Walk 27).

31 ELEFTHERNA (map page 132, photograph page 131)

🚗 by car: under 10min-1h45min on foot. Park at Eleftherna. Follow Walk 31 (page 130) and picnic at the Byzantine tower shown on page 131, or continue along this fascinating walk as long as you like. The riverbed reached in 1h is a particularly pleasant setting.

🚌 by bus to Eleftherna; then see notes for motorists above.

CT4 MONI GOUVERNETO
(touring map and map page 71, photograph page 26)

🚗 by car: about 5-10min on foot. Follow Car tour 4 to the Gouverneto Monastery and park. There are good picnic places on the hillside below the monastery, overlooking the sea, but little shade.

CT6 KOURTALIOTIKO GORGE (touring map)

🚗 by car: 5min down on foot; 10min back up. Follow Car tour 6 from Asomatos (page 31). *Note:* If you're based at Plakias, this picnic is also accessible by 🚌; ask for the Kourtaliotiko Gorge and waterfall.

CT8 AMARI VALLEY (touring map, photograph page 10)

🚗 by car: under 5min on foot. Follow Car tour 8, page 36, to cross the River Platys (125.5km). Park well off the road and picnic by the bridge.

A country code for walkers and motorists

A country code for walkers and motorists

Observance of certain unwritten rules is essential when out walking or driving in the countryside anywhere, but particularly on Crete's rugged terrain, where irresponsible behaviour can lead to dangerous mistakes. Whether you are an experienced rambler or not, it is important to adhere to a country code, to avoid causing damage, harming animals, or even endangering your own life.

- **Do not take risks.** Do not attempt walks beyond your capacity, and do not wander off the paths described if there is any sign of enveloping cloud or if it is late in the day.
- **Do not walk alone** and *always* tell someone exactly where you are going and what time you plan to return. On any but a very short walk near to villages, be sure to take a compass, whistle, torch, extra water and warm clothing, as well as some high energy food, like chocolate. This may sound 'over the top' to an inexperienced walker, but it could save your life.
- **Do not light fires**; everything gets tinder dry. If you smoke, make absolutely sure cigarettes are completely extinguished.
- **Do not frighten animals.** The goats and sheep you may encounter are not used to strangers. By making a noise, trying to touch or photograph them, you may cause them to run in fear and be hurt.
- **Walk quietly** through all farms, hamlets and villages, and **leave all gates just as you found them**, wherever they are. Although animals may not be in evidence, the gates *do* have a purpose — generally to keep grazing or herded goats or sheep in (or out of) an area.
- **Protect all wild and cultivated plants**. Don't pick fruit; it is somebody else's livelihood! You'll doubtless be offered some en route, anyhow. Avoid walking over cultivated land.
- **Take all your litter away with you**.
- When driving, **never block roads or tracks**. Park where you will not inconvenience anyone or cause danger.

Goat pen near Rodopos (Walk 11)

✸ Touring

Crete is a very large island, and most visitors hire a car for some part of their stay to get to grips with it. It pays to hire for a minimum of three days and, although you may find cheaper rates with small companies, do think what you're paying for with the better-known firms. The larger companies offer the advantage of representation all over the island. Since it's likely that you'll want to cover a lot of ground, you'll be in a better position hiring from a well-known company, should anything go wrong en route.

Remember that tyres are *not* covered by insurance; you won't be charged for a simple puncture, but ruined tyres will have to be paid for. Check the car before you set off, and make sure you've got a spare and a jack (often under the bonnet). Be sure, too, that you understand the terms of the hire contract you have signed (of course this should be available in English). Keep your car hire contract and driving licence with you at all times when out on the road. It's worth taking note of the car hire company's telephone numbers as well, just in case ...

Our car touring notes are brief; they include little information readily available in standard guidebooks — or the handouts you can obtain free from tourist offices at home and tourist information kiosks on the island itself. Instead, we've concentrated on the 'logistics' of touring: times and distances, road conditions, and giving clear directions where you might falter or be misled using other existing maps. Most of all, we emphasise possibilities for **walking** (if you team up with walkers you may lower your car rental costs) and **picnicking**. The symbol *P* advises you of a picnic spot; see pages 10-12. While some of the suggestions for short walks and picnics may not be suitable during a long car tour, you may find a landscape that you would like to explore at leisure another day.

The large colour touring map is designed to be held out opposite the touring notes and contains all the information you will need outside the towns.* The tours have Hania as their departure/return point, but they could quite easily be joined from other centres. Plans of Hania and Rethimnon, with city exits, are on pages 8 and 9.

*The *reverse* shows walks and tours in *Landscapes of Eastern Crete.*

Some points worth noting

We cannot stress too strongly the advantage of taking with you one of the books mentioned on page 6, detailing Crete's history and archaeological heritage. Note also:

■ While there are plenty of **petrol** stations on the island, it still pays to fill up at the start of a journey, especially if you are going to spend time off the beaten track.

■ **Allow plenty of time for visits**; the times we give for the tours include only very brief stops at viewpoints labelled (☎) in the notes.

■ **Telephones** are located at most kiosks, at OTE (telephone exchanges) and in cafeneions.

■ Don't be flummoxed by **Greek road signs**; they are almost invariably followed by English ones.

■ You are meant to cross a **solid white line near the edge of the road**, when someone wants to overtake. However, beware of slower vehicles, laden donkeys, bikes, etc ahead, when you round corners.

■ Conversely, **a solid white line in the middle of the road** means NO OVERTAKING — regardless of the behaviour of other motorists who appear not to notice it.

■ Do think before you pull up to admire a view, if you are not at a **viewpoint** with parking; remember that other motorists cannot see round corners.

■ Never throw **cigarette ends** out of the car.

■ Come to a standstill at **stop signs**.

■ **The spelling of village names may vary**. We have used the letter 'H' where an 'X' or 'CH' might be used locally; this is to aid pronunciation.

■ In towns, only **park your car** where permitted.

■ **Priority signs** (red/black/white arrows) on narrow stretches of road give priority to the *black arrow.*

■ You will see roadside shrines (little boxes, perhaps filled with a cross, a candle, an icon, pictures, etc). They are a sad warning that at sometime in the past a fatal accident involving vehicles has occurred at that spot. **Drive carefully**.

Distances quoted are *cumulative kilometres* from Hania. A key to the symbols in the notes is on the touring map. Note that only the largest churches — or churches that are landmarks — are highlighted, since every village has at least one church! The same can be said of tavernas or cafeneions; you should be able to find some sustenance almost anywhere en route.

All motorists should read the country code on page 13 and go quietly in the countryside. *Kalo taxidi!*

1 THE FAR WEST

Hania • (Kastelli) • (Polirinia) • Sfinari • Vathi • Moni Chrisoskalitisas • (Elafonisi) • Elos • Topolia • Hania

170km/105mi; about 5 hours 15 minutes' driving; Exit B from Hania (see town plan page 8)

On route: Picnics (see pages 10-12): (13), 14; Walks 1, (11), (12), (13), 14, 15, (18)

All roads are quite good. The national road running along the north coast of the island has one section yet to be completed (at press date) — from Galatas, just west of Hania, to Kolimbari. The section from Kolimbari to Kastelli avoids Kallergiana, Kaloudiana and Drapanias.

You can drive miles through this wild, rugged western end of Crete and see virtually no-one; on this tour, you're alone in the landscape, once you leave the north coast road. The sea views are dramatic on the coastal drive and contrast well with the countryside inland on the return journey. Try to set off early in the morning, so you have time for a detour to the turquoise shallows at Elafonisi.

From 1866 Square, take Exit B (Skalidi/Kissamou). This one-way system is signposted 'Omalos/Kastellion'. There are plenty of petrol stations along this north coast road, so fill up (⛽) before turning off. Pass the turning for Omalos at traffic lights (2km) and continue west. All the beach-side villages on this route —

Here and page 16: the essence of Crete

Galatas, Kalamaki, Glaros, Kato Stalos (where Walk 1 begins and ends), **Agia Marina** (△), **Platanias** — have tavernas and rooms and apartments for rent (🏨🏠△✕).

Cross the Keritis River (12km) and drive on (🚰 13.6km), flanked by orange groves and large patches of bamboo (🚰 15.5km). Soon the route passes through **Maleme** (16km 🏨✕🚰). The village saw violent activity during the Second World War; it was here that the Battle of Crete flared up. A signpost on the left (17km), in German and Greek, indicates the German war graves.

Continue along the north coast, hemming the sea. You will see the Rodopou Peninsula (Walks 11 and 12) lunging out ahead in the middle distance. Drive through **Tavronitis** (19.5km ✕🚰). **Kamisiana** (20.5km ✕) and **Rapaniana** (21km 🏕🏨✕🚰) flash by. On your way through **Skoutelonas** (22km), look to the right, at the beginning of the peninsula, to see Moni Gonia (Walk 12). There is a junction of roads at **Kolimbari** by the Hotel Rosmarie (where Walk 12 ends). The turning right goes into Kolimbari and to the Gonia Monastery — see them at leisure another day, or plan to do Walk 12, which comes down into the middle of Kolimbari. Go straight across at the junction, making for Kastelli-Kissamou. Then fork right, onto the last section of the national road. After 1.5km pass a turn to Rodopos, where both Walks 11 and 12 start. Soon the Gramvousa Peninsula is clearly visible (see below) and you are on the outskirts of Kastelli.

Detour: If you wish to make a detour to the site at Polirinia, look out at 40.5km for the turn-off left — it's just beyond the OTE, at a junction with a central triangle, opposite a petrol station (🚰). There is a small sign up on a wall (in Greek), indicating Polirinia. You'll pass a new church on the left and continue inland, passing another sign for Polirinia at 42km. Drive with care along this potholed asphalt road. Go through Karfiana and Grigoriana before coming to Polirinia★ (47km 🏛✕). Drive to the end of the road and park near the taverna. Walk 13 ends here; if you'd like to stretch your legs, you could

17

follow some of the walk in reverse, to the pleasant picnic spot illustrated on page 79 (Picnic 13; notes page 12).

The main tour bypasses the Polirinia turn-off and Kastelli-Kissamou★ (**⚓▲✖🚲M**), by continuing on the main road. Kastelli is certainly worth visiting — it has a pleasant atmosphere — but we suggest you come on another day, when you will have time to combine a visit with a walk or even the detour to Polirinia and a swim at Falasarna's beach (mentioned below). Staying on the main road, pass a small harbour and then the Kissamou port. The Gramvousa Peninsula spreads before you directly to the right, a brown-grey mound disappearing into the sea. At 52km a road (rough for the last kilometre) leads down right to Falasarna★ (**⚓**), where there is a good sandy beach — if you feel you have time for a swim. However, it will make your day very long to detour at this stage. If you decide to go for a swim, take the Elafonisi detour later in the day.

So keep up on the main road and head round left into Platanos, a long strung-out village. There's a good view back over the beach at 56km (📷); you can also see the tip of Falasarna. Then pass another good viewpoint at 58km (📷), over the Bay of Sfinari. In **Sfinari** (62km ✖) we turn away from the sea and head up into the hills. The road passes through the tiny hamlet of **Ano Sfinari** (64km) and winds along beside a ravine, rounding its end at 66km. Between **Kambos** (70km) and **Keramoti**, a village that juts out off the hillside, there is a steepish drop down to the sea. The village of **Amigdalokefali** is set mostly below the road, and then you pass through **Simadi** (81km), **Papadiana** (83km) and **Kefali** (85km ✖).

Half a kilometre beyond Kefali, turn right on a road

that descends through tree-covered hillsides to **Vathi** (87km). Keep right at Vathi on the rough road to Chriso-skalitisas. Go through **Plokamiana** and by 93.5km you can at last see the monastery ahead with its bright blue roof. Turn left round the Bay of Stomio. An ugly rash of houses has sprung up at **Chrisoskalitisas** (95km ✕), just a kilometre from the monastery★ itself (96km ⚐). Having visited the church, you're ready to start the return journey. But first, if you fancy a break and a swim, take the route going off right 0.5km past the monastery, signposted Elafonisi. It leads to a lovely sandy beach and turquoise water — protected and created by the nearby Elafonisi Islands. Walk 18 can end at Elafonisi or the monastery.

Retracing the route from Chrisoskalitisas, turn right onto the asphalt road at 107.5km (signposted to Elos). Past **Louhi** (110km), keep to the main road, curving round to the right at **Limni** (111km) and going into **Elos** (111.5km ✕⚐), a pretty village strung out through chestnut trees. Keep straight on at **Mili** (116km) and look out for any traffic coming in from the right (from Paleohora). Leave **Katsomatados** (Picnic 14; Walks 14 and 15) off to the right at 119.5km. Soon you will have a wonderful view through the Topolia Gorge★ (120.5km 📷). Just past this obvious viewpoint, there is an old sign at the left of the road indicating the cave chapel of Agia Sophia★ (⚐⚐) up on the hillside. Go through the narrow tunnel in the gorge wall — headlights on and hooting. Then continue through the pretty hillside village of **Topolia** (122.5km), where Walk 15 ends, and **Voulgaro** (125.5km ⚐), where Walk 14 ends. Reaching the main coast road at **Kaloudiana** (130km ⚐), turn right and make your way back onto the national road at Koleni, for the return to Hania (170km).

A mesmerising turquoise lagoon, fringed with bleached white sand, and one of the islands off the shore at Gramvousa. A good track now extends almost to the end of the peninsula. From the end of the track you could follow a path to the far northwest corner of Crete and enjoy a swim. There's no shade, so do remember to take a sunhat! Gramvousa is easily reached from Car tour 1.

2 PALEOHORA AND SOUTH COAST BEACHES

Hania • Tavronitis • Voukolies • Kandanos • Paleohora
• Kandanos • (Sougia) • Hania
152km/94mi; 4 hours' driving; Exit B from Hania (town plan page 8)
On route: Picnics (see pages 10-12): (17); Walks 1, 17, (18)
All roads are good.

You will see two coasts on this trip — the north coast, which you follow out of Hania, and the south coast at Paleohora, where there is a long beach stretching for miles east and west. The route cuts straight across the island from north to south — climbing up through hillside villages that saw action during the Second World War — as far as Kandanos, before descending again through the district of Selinos — a region rich in Byzantine churches housing a host of frescoes. You might like to make a detour to Anidri, where there is a church of particular interest.

Leave Hania by Exit B, following Car tour 1 as far as **Tavronitis** (19.5km). Here take the left turn signposted to Paleohora and Kandanos. Pass through **Neranztia** (23.5km; 🛋 at 25.5km) and, in **Voukolies** (26km), go through the main square. Head up right, climbing out of this large village and the valley. Wind up through olive trees into the high hills. By about 33km you can see over the sea to the west coast on your right. Then, at **Dromonero** (34km), the countryside opens out, and you enjoy some very fine views. Driving through the spread-out village of **Kakopetros** (38km), follow the road curving round to the right, signposted to Paleohora. Catch your last glimpse of the north coast — with the Gramvousa Peninsula, shown on pages 18-19, jutting out into the sea. The rockier landscape here is somewhat softened by horse chestnut trees. **Mesavlia** (43.5km) is just a few houses, followed by **Floria** (47km) and **Anavanos**. At the end of the village of **Kandanos** (56km ✝🛋), follow the road round to the right and head south.

Cross a stream at **Plemeniana** (58km; Agios Georgios ✝ with 15th-century frescoes). Further on, more frescoes merit a visit, in **Kakodiki** (63km ✝). Beyond here (at 64km), you can make a short detour left to Agia Tria — just 2km return — to see the frescoed chapel of Mikhail Arkhangelos (✝; the key is with the priest who lives further up the hill). Continuing south, go through **Vlithias** (67km). Soon the sea and the south coast come into view. Pass through **Kalamos** and **Ligia**, and then a rocky valley.

Paleohora (73.5km 🚹△✖🛋) is approached along an avenue of eucalyptus trees. At 74km, pass the turn-off for

Anidri★, which you might like to visit to see the 14th-century frescoes in Agios Georgios church (✝). If so, take the turn and fork left again at the sea; turn right at the Paleohora Club, then left at a sign 'Camping'. The main tour passes the Anidri turn-off and comes into Paleohora. Turn left just before the road narrows; you can see the clock tower ahead. Park on the sea-side esplanade. Walk 17, from Sougia via the site at Lisos, ends here, and Walk 18 to Elafonisi begins a taxi ride from here.

The simplest way to return to Hania is to retrace your outgoing route. However, if you have decided to cover a lot of ground, it's possible to include Sougia in today's tour (add an extra hour). If you opt for this excursion, follow the road back as far as Kandanos (this is really the *best* route, unless you have a four-wheel drive vehicle and can easily bump along the unsurfaced routes via Azogires and Anidri). In Kandanos, once past the square, turn right opposite the ✆ for Temenia; this road leads south via Anisaraki. In Temenia, pass the turning right (one of the mostly rough routes from Paleohora) and, a kilometre beyond Temenia, at a junction, go left (signposted to Rodovani). Go through Maza, following a rough road through a gorge (📷) down to the sea. When you meet the main Hania/Sougia road, go right and start heading downhill to the coast. There's a good view of the towering wall of the White Mountains ahead of you as you descend. Drive through Moni and on to Sougia. To return from Sougia, pick up Car tour 3 at the 67km-point (page 23).

The oleander-bright gorge at Sougia (Walk 17 and Picnic 17)

3 COUNTRYSIDE, COASTAL BACKWATER AND HIGH CRETAN PASTURELAND

Hania • Nea Roumata • Agia Irini • Epanohori • Sougia • Omalos • Lakki • Fournes • Hania

159km/99mi; under 4 hours' driving; Exit B from Hania (plan page 8)

On route: Picnics (see pages 10-12): (1), (2), 17; Walks 2, 16, 17, 19-21

A wide new road crosses the Omalos; only a very short stretch was still unsurfaced at the end of 1996. Coming back down from Omalos you are likely to meet coaches — patience and care are required.

This tour takes a very picturesque route through wooded valleys and the Agia Irini Gorge to Sougia, a pleasant backwater. En route one or some of your company might like to walk down the gorge (Walk 16) and meet up in Sougia. At Sougia, you may like to do the very attractive walk along another gorge to the site at Lisos, and then swim in the lovely clear water from Sougia's pebbly beach, before heading into the hills. The stretch to Omalos on the return journey is one of the most beautiful parts of the tour. So even if you're not going to 'walk Samaria', this tour will take you to the top — where shepherds gather on the plain and eagles and vultures soar overhead.

Fill up with petrol before you leave Hania by Exit B (Skalidi/Kissamou). Turn left at 2km, immediately past the narrow bridge, following signposting for Alikianos and Omalos. Drive through the suburb of **Vamvakopoulo** (☎) and then **Agia** (10km), setting for Walk 1 and Picnic 1. Continue until you see the right turn (12km ☎) for Alikianos and Skines (opposite a ☎ and a war memorial). Take this turn and cross the bridge over the Keritis River. The road bypasses both Alikianos and Skines. Once through **Hilaro** (20km) it won't be long before you are driving through wooded valleys, planted with citrus trees. The road starts to climb seriously (22km) and becomes more twisty as it leads through the foothills of the White Mountains. Pass through **Nea Roumata** (29.5km) and **Prases** (30km ✝✗). Glorious hillsides surround you now — covered in chestnut, fig, olive, walnut and plane trees ... to name but a few. Pass the turning left for Omalos (38.5km).

Just beyond this turning, the Agia Irini Valley begins on the left; it runs through a gorge and down to the Libyan Sea, emerging at Sougia. Enter **Agia Irini** (42km; ☎ at 43km, not open Sundays). After you leave this village (a sign tells you so at 44km), watch for a board on the left announcing the Irini Gorge (Walk 16) — you may like to park there and enjoy a picnic in the pines.

Pass through **Epanohori** (45.5km), from where you will have a first glimpse of the Libyan Sea, and start heading down to Sougia — via **Prines**, **Tsiskiana** and **Kambanos** (52km), beyond which the road swings round left and continues through **Maralia** and **Agriles** (56km; 🏪, not on Sundays). Turn left at the T-junction one kilometre past Agriles (Paleohora is off to the right — 22km of rough road away). In a kilometre or two you will have a splendid view over the valley and down to the sea, tucked neatly into the V ahead. **Moni** is the last village before **Sougia** (67km). Walk 16 ends in this backwater, and Walk 17 begins here. The setting for Picnic 17, shown on page 21, is only 10-15 minutes away on foot.

Head back from Sougia the same way and after 29km

Walk 21: The Samaria Gorge is western Crete's most famous walk. Here are the Sideroportes — the 'Iron Gates', where the gorge is at its most narrow, and the rock walls soar up about 600m (2000ft) on either side.

take the turning for Omalos passed earlier. The road goes by a small white church on the right some 9km along, as you drive through a pass. Keep right at a fork by a cafeneion sign; by now you will be on the **Omalos**. When you reach the road which leads along the side of the plain to the top of the Samaria Gorge, turn right and drive to **Xiloskala** at the top of the ravine. From here you can look down into the gorge itself (Walk 21) and up to Gingilos Mountain (Walk 19; photographs pages 93 and 95). You'll also see the route up to the mountain refuge at Kallergi, which we follow at the start of Walk 20. We hope this panorama will inspire you to walk!

From Xiloskala keep on the main road back to Hania, about an hour's drive away. You pass a taverna and rooms for rent (▲✖) at the edge of the plain. Coach groups stop here for breakfast, en route for Samaria. Leave the plain behind and start to descend towards the distant coast. The most noticeable place on the return route is **Lakki** (127km ✚✖), shown below. Walk 2 ends in this village. Take care past here to keep to the road, as it swings round to the right (132km) near the turning to Askordalos. Drive into **Fournes**, go over the bridge and curve left through the village (a right turn leads to Meskla, another village visited in Walk 2). Pass the junction to Alikianos, and go straight on (🚌 145km), to meet the main north coast road after 12km. Turn right to Hania (159km).

4 THE AKROTIRI PENINSULA

Hania • Kounoupidiana • Stavros • Agia Triada • Moni Gouverneto • (Souda Bay Cemetery) • Hania

50km/31mi; 1 hour 45 minutes' driving; Exit C from Hania (plan page 8)
On route: Picnic (see pages 10-12): CT4; Walk 10
Except for the access roads to the monasteries and the last stretch of road to Stavros, roads are in good condition. Note: The Gouverneto Monastery is closed from 14.00-17.00, but the powers that be often close from 12.00. Men should wear trousers and women longish skirts.

The Akrotiri Peninsula, mushrooming out into the sea northeast of Hania, invites exploration. You may have seen some of it if you flew into Hania's airport, but you won't have seen any of the peninsula's treasures. The ruins of what is purported to be the island's earliest monastery are accessible by foot from this tour — as well as two other monasteries. All three are in lovely, peaceful settings. With splendid views and swimming possibilities, this short tour could well fill a whole day very pleasantly.

Leave Hania by Exit C: 1.5km from the market, follow the road round to the right, just beyond the Doma Hotel. The road is signposted for Akrotiri and the airport. It climbs up out of Hania, leaving the old part of the town (Halepa) off to the left. The left turn you need to take to get out onto the peninsula is indicated by two signposts (5km): the first is for the Venizelos' Graves and the second for Kounoupidiana. It's an odd junction; take what appears to be the second road left, then go immediately right at

Left: Lakki (Car tour 3 and Walk 2). Below: Stavros, where the mountain falls into the sea and the beach is perfect for a swim and a picnic. 'Zorba the Greek' was filmed here.

*Moni Gouverneto
(Walk 10 and
Picnic CT4)*

the T-junction (signposted 'Kounoupidiana'). But for a
wonderful view of Hania, first turn *left* instead of right at
this T-junction and drive for two minutes to the Venizelos'
Graves, where you can gaze down over the town, the
north coast, and Theodorou Island beyond (📷).

Back on the car tour route, very soon after the junction,
you will have another splendid view (📷) across Akrotiri
to Stavros, where the mountain falls away into the sea.
Coming to a fork (7km 🅿), take the right arm, then keep
left and start heading downhill, through **Kounoupidiana**
(✕). As you leave the village, turn left at 8km for Stavros.
Kalathas Beach (9km ✕) is passed, followed by **Horafakia**. About 0.5km beyond the latter, turn left for Stavros.
Three kilometres further on, turn right at a junction and
come into **Stavros** (✕); the lovely beach, shown on page
25, is perfect for swimming and picnicking.

Now head back the way you came, as far as the fork
in Horafakia (20km). Instead of going right, back to Hania,
take the left-hand turning (signposted ΑΓ ΤΡΙΑΔΑ). At the
next fork (20.5km) keep going round at the sign for
Gouverneto, heading towards the mast on the hill ahead.
Turn left at the next set of signs (23.5km) — one pointing
in the direction you've come from Horafakia, the other
the back of the Agia Triada/Gouverneto sign. Drive down
the avenue of trees into **Agia Triada** (24km ⛪✕).

After visiting the monastery★, head on to Gouverneto,
four kilometres away. With your back to Agia Triada, go
right. A sign for Gouverneto (ΓΟΥΒΕΡΝΕΤΟ) takes you into
a right turn at 25km. Apart from visiting **Moni Gouver-
neto★** (29km ⛪), why not picnic on the nearby slopes or
walk down to the ancient Katholikou Monastery (Walk 10)?

Return to Agia Triada and, at the junction beyond the
monastery (34km), bear left to Hania. A kilometre further
on, turn right; the road, signposted to Hania, curves round
to the left. Half a kilometre along, turn right and then right
again (38km). Where the road divides above Souda Bay
(43km), either go left and down via the Souda Bay Cemetery and Souda or continue straight to Hania (50km).

5 THE FOOTHILLS OF THE LEVKA ORI (THE WHITE MOUNTAINS)

Hania • Aptera • Katohori • Kambi • Mournies • Hania

67km/42mi; 2 hours' driving; Exit A from Hania (town plan page 8)

On route: Picnics (see pages 10-12): 3a, 3b, 4; Walks (2), 3, 4

Reasonable to good roads; some potholes between Katohori and Kambi.

History and hills combine nicely on this tour, which is a short spin into the lovely countryside inland from Hania. With the wild flowers of spring, the stillness of high summer or the colours of autumn, it's a pleasant morning or afternoon circuit. You'll drive to the fringe of the Levka Ori — often snow-capped until mid-summer.

Leave Hania by Exit A (Apokoronou). At the end of this tree-lined avenue (🚗) leading away from the town, follow the road round to the right (Souda is straight on) and, moments later, turn left onto the main highway, signposted to Rethimnon. Make the first move off the beaten track by turning right for Aptera at 12km. At the junction in **Megala Horafia** (13km), turn hard left; after one kilometre, you will see **Aptera★** (🏛) spread out to the right. Drive on to the Turkish fort perched up in a commanding position over Souda Bay (15km 📷).

From the fort go back to the junction in Megala Horafia and turn sharp left for Stilos, heading down through undulating hills. Make another sharp turn, this time to the right, at 20km. Beyond **Malaxa**, at 29km, turn left for Kontopoula (signposted Κοντοπουλα). (Turning *right* at this point, you would find a good taverna with magnificent views a minute away; ✖📷.) Head on to **Kontopoula** — a gorgeous panorama of hills and mountains is ahead of you. The next collection of houses on the route is **Katohori** (34km). At the far end of this village, turn left over the bridge. Walk 3 starts here, and you can park here for Picnic 3a or 3b (photograph page 51). Make for **Kambi** (Καμπι; 38km) and take the right-hand fork into the village square. The church and a cafeneion are on the right. Walk 4 and Picnic 4 are based here.

Return the way you came; beyond the bridge at Katohori turn left instead of right. At the junction in **Gerolakos** (47km) turn right (a left turn leads to Drakonas; Alternative walk 2). Past **Loulos**, **Aletrouvari** and **Panagia** (where you pass a war memorial on the left), the route curves down the side of a steep valley, through **Vantes** and **Mournies** (62km). At 64km turn left and go straight over at the next crossroads (66km). Straight over again at the next lights — and soon come to Hania's market (67km).

6 A SLICE OF CRETE

Hania • Vrises • Askyfou • Hora Sfakion • Frango-kastello • Selia • Asomatos • Moni Preveli • Rethimnon • Episkopi • Georgioupoli • Hania

240km/149mi (via the old road from Rethimnon); 223km/138mi (via the new road from Rethimnon); 6-7 hours' driving; Exit A from Hania (town plan page 8)

On route: Picnics (see pages 10-12): 6, (8a, 8b), 25, 27, CT6; Walks 5, 6, 8, (9), 24, 25, 26, 27

The road south, although it has undergone widening, is a mass of tortuous loops. Special care is needed when taking bends or overtaking (if you ever get the chance), because there are a lot of buses and coaches on this route. Fortunately their drivers are experienced! Note: Moni Preveli is open from 08.00-13.00 and from 15.00 to 18.00; men should wear trousers and women longish skirts.

You'll sample a bit of everything on this tour, which encompasses a neat square of the island. First we head south, following the same route thousands of retreating, war-weary Antipodean and British soldiers trudged over during World War II. We call in at the pretty harbour village of Hora Sfakion, from where boats ply west to Loutro, Agia Roumeli at the foot of the Samaria Gorge, and Paleohora. We turn east, following the coast to Frangokastello, a solitary landmark, once a fortified castle. Past the Kotsifas Gorge, we visit one of Crete's most beautiful monasteries, Moni Preveli, set in glorious solitude. Heading north, we leave the views over the Libyan Sea, following the Kourtaliotiko Gorge to Rethimnon. Here it's really worth getting out of the car to walk down to a magical spot where there is a waterfall and a small church tucked away. From there it's back to base — either via the old country road or along the direct national road.

Take Exit A out of Hania (Apokoronou), heading east on the main coast road and leaving Souda down to the left. Pass the turning off to Aptera★ (12km; Car tour 5). At 31km turn right towards Vrises. Turn left almost immediately at the junction and enter **Vrises**. Turn left in the village (signposted Sfakia) and head south, with the magnificent White Mountains lying to the right. You pass the left turn to Alikampos (37km), where Walk 6 starts.

The road twists uphill, and the landscape becomes rockier and greyer with the climb. There's a splendid sight as you round a corner (47km 🔂): the plain of Askyfou, shown on page 112, spreads out across to the left of the road. A striking Turkish fort sits on a mound in the foreground. **Kares** (48km) is the little village on the hillock down to the left; Walk 26 starts here. The road hems the plain, and the next village is the main one of the area, **Askyfou** itself (49km ▣). Drive on round the plain and then follow the road as it heads south again. This is the route that thousands of soldiers from Britain, Australia and New Zealand took when fleeing western Crete.

   The road skirts the Imbros Gorge, which you see down left at 55km. Walk 25 starts here; a twenty-minute walk

Georgioupoli: a peaceful sight at the end of a rocky breakwater which protects the town beach to the right and the small harbour to the left.

from **Imbros** would take you to the setting for Picnic 25. Shortly (at 59km), if you look left again, you can see along the south coast to the east — including Frangokastello. But you are still high up above the sea for the time being; you still have to drive carefully as the road snakes its way down to the coast in tortuous loops. At 68km, the coast road comes in from the east. Continue down and on into the pretty village shown on page 110, **Hora Sfakion★** (72km ▲ ✕). As you curve down into the village, take the lower road to the harbour. Walks 21-25 finish at Hora Sfakion — by boat or on foot.

Head back out the way you came in and reach a fork at 75km. Follow signs for Patsianos, carrying straight on along the coast. Pass through **Komitades** (76km); Walk 25 — which started out at Imbros — can end here at Komitades, or at Hora Sfakion. Continue on through **Vraskas, Vouvas, Nomikiana** and **Agios Nektarios** (where Walk 26 ends); then turn right at 83km for Frangokastello, heading down towards the sea. Four kilometres of rough road carry you to **Frangokastello★** (87km ⚔). After wandering round the ruined castle, carry on along the same coast road, still heading east. Turn right at the junction (90km), where there is a signpost for **Skaloti**. Drive through that village and on to **Argoules**. Cross a stream and come into **Ano Rodakino** and **Kato Rodakino** (100km).

Beyond the right-hand turn to Koraka Beach, the views are well worth stopping to admire. There is a particularly good viewpoint looking back west along the coast at 103km, and you can park at 104km to admire the panorama (📷): steep cliffs plunge down to the sea on your right, and the inland landscape is dramatically rocky and barren. A few kilometres further on you have wonderful views in all directions, with the peaks of hills jutting up all round ... but nowhere to park the car.

The road bends down through **Selia** (111km). At 112km, take the sharp right-hand turn downhill (the road from Rethimnon, which follows the Kotsifas Gorge). From **Mirthios** (114km 📷✕) there is a fine view over Plakias. Turn left at the junction (115km), where a sign indicates 'Plakias 3km right'. (But turn right if you wish to go to Plakias Beach — for a swim or a taverna lunch.) Then pass **Mariou**, set well up away from the sea; flat, cultivated land is on your right.

If you decide not to visit the Preveli Monastery (which would be a great pity), you will find Rethimnon signposted

Chapel at Anopolis (Walk 23). This stunning setting could be reached via a short detour from Hora Sfakion.

at **Asomatos** (122km 🚌), where Walk 27 begins (and where you can park for Picnic 27). Here the main tour turns down sharp right into a bend; you will be heading almost back on yourself (there is a signpost here for the monastery and Lefkogia). After 123km turn left onto a tarmac road and follow it all the way to the monastery. To the left you see the Kourtaliotiko Gorge. Pass the ruins of the original 16th-century monastery★ and keep on the road. Soon, just round a corner, over the hill, **Moni Preveli★** (129km ✝) comes into view. The setting is beautiful and very peaceful. The palm-fringed beach where the Megalopotamos River opens out into the sea, and the monastery, are shown on pages 118-119. Walk 27 makes a superb, if rather long, circuit from Asomatos to Preveli.

The tour continues from Preveli by retracing the route, past the original monastery and back to the bridge, where you turn right (133km) and rejoin the main road (135km). Back in **Asomatos**, turn right (136km), following signs to Rethimnon. This route takes you along the Kourtaliotiko Gorge for a short way. Look out for railings and small signs; just before them, there is a place to park on the right. Do make the effort to walk down — and back up — here. If you're lucky there won't be a coachload of other visitors. The path leads to a well-placed church and a splashing cool waterfall (Picnic CT6).

From here head north. The countryside opens out at **Koxare** (143km). When you meet the main Rethimnon/Agia Galini road (144km), turn left (🚌 151km). Pass a turning left to Hora Sfakion and continue into **Armeni** (157km 🚌). Before long the sea and the north coast are in sight in the distance and, as you approach Rethimnon, there is a very good view over the town and the new harbour (📷). To explore **Rethimnon★** (167km 🍴 ▲ ✖ 🍴 ⊕M) go under the national road and follow the road round, first to the left and then to the right, to park in the town centre (plan page 9). The old harbour is a good place to stretch your legs. More than any other town on Crete, this still speaks of its medieval past, with its Ottoman and Venetian buildings. The museum houses a collection of coins and antiquities.

Leaving Rethimnon, make your way back onto the national road or, if you've still got some energy, follow us: go under the national road at the west end of Rethimnon and head south in the direction of Atsipopoulo (171km). You will drive through **Atsipopoulo**, **Prines**, **Gonia** and **Agios Andreas** in quick succession. They are country villages set along a wooded valley. **Episkopi** (189km 🍴) is rather larger. Just past the turning to Φιλακι (Filaki), look straight ahead, and you will see a low dip, with mountains receding behind it. Walk 6 brings you down there on your descent from Alikampos to Kournas.

Go left (193km) towards Kournas, turning onto a dirt road that heads inland. Keep straight on when Filaki is indicated left again. There is a pretty church at the beginning of **Kournas** village (196km ✝📷). Climb up through the village square, leaving a new church on your right. As you leave Kournas, you will see the north coast again, and then Crete's only freshwater lake will come into view below — a lovely, invigorating sight (198km; Picnic 6).

Pass the end of the lake and follow signs to Hania, passing the end of Walk 6 at 201km. Turn left for Hania at the junction (203km) and cross over the main east/west national road to come into the main square of **Georgiou-poli** (204km ▲ ✖). Walk 5 makes a pleasing circuit from this village to Selia and back (photographs pages 29, 56 and 61). Turn left in front of the kiosk and go down an avenue of eucalyptus trees. The main road runs along to the left of this country road. Turn left at 210km to join the main road (there is no signposting, but there is a solitary building on the right). Turn right for Hania. Pass the Venetian fort that is now a prison known by its Turkish name, Itzedin, and continue to Hania (240km). It's much easier to get into the centre of town if you leave the national road where Souda is indicated right (*not* the ferry terminal, which comes up first) — then turn left at the junction and go back to town the way you came out.

7 CRETAN TREASURES

Hania • (Rethimnon) • Armeni • Spili • Agia Galini • Festos • Agia Triada • Hania

264km/164mi; about 6 hours' driving; Exit A from Hania (see town plan page 8)

On route: Picnics (see pages 10-12): (8a, 8b); Walks 8 and 9 are nearby

This route follows major roads all the way. But never assume there won't be any potholes; subsidence on the southbound stretch has left damage you'will have to reckon with when driving.

Well, this *is* a long haul, but it takes in a very large slice of Cretan landscape on the way to its goals, Festos and Agia Triada. We've included it because we are sure that many of you will want to make the effort to see two of Crete's major sites, even though you are based in western Crete. To reach our destination, we travel via Spili — an exceedingly picturesque spot — and then between Mt Kedros and Siderotas.

Leave Hania by Exit A (Apokoronou). At the end of the tree-lined avenue (🚑) leading away from the town, follow the road round to the right at 6km (Souda will be signposted straight on). Moments later, turn left onto the national road, signposted for Rethimnon. Pass the turnings for Aptera★ (Car tour 5), Vrises and Hora Sfakion (30km; Tour 6), and Georgioupoli (33km; also Tour 6). The road runs directly along by the sea from here to Rethimnon (🚑 at 41 km; ✗🚑 at 48km). You will have a good view of Rethimnon from the outskirts and then go through traffic lights (59km; a left turn here leads to the Old Harbour; a right to Atsipopoulo). Leave the national road at the next route sign, where Spili and Armeni are signposted off to the right.

Head south now, through **Armeni** (70km 🚑 and nearby Minoan cemetery **⌂★**), **Mixorouma** (86km 🚑) and **Spili** (89km **▲✗**), a large and pretty village well worth a 'pit stop'. Continue via **Kisou Kampos** (95km 🚑), and

Agia Galini is a very popular tourist centre, so try to visit out of season. From this charming port there are views north to the Ida Range (Psiloritis).

watch out for road subsidence around **Akoumia** (98km), where the road doubles back on itself briefly. Look up to Psiloritis — which is quite likely to be snow-capped until high summer. Take a moment, too, to admire the whole Ida range (📷), with Mt Kedros in the foreground.

Take the turning to **Agia Galini** at 112km. The road divides: go left and drive down to the harbour of this busy resort (114km 🏨 ✕ 🚌). Having stretched your legs, head back to the main road. Turn right at the junction, following signposting to Iraklion (△✕ at 116km). At 122km you drive into the county of Iraklion, past a mass of plastic greenhouses, and then on via the ugly, functional spread of **Timbaki** (127km 🚌). Before long you will see a sign in Greek and then a sign in English indicating that Festos is 2km ahead and Agia Triada 5km.

The Minoan site of **Festos★** (129km ⊓✕WC) is in a glorious position — with views towards the Dikti and Lasithi mountains to the east, the Ida range to the north, and the Asterousias to the south. From Festos, carry on through the car park and fork right. This turning takes you back towards the Mesara Plain, to a spot from which you can walk down to **Agia Triada★** (132km ⊓) in a few minutes. The remains of this Minoan summer palace are also in a delightful setting.

When it's time to head for home, simply retrace the route back to Hania. If you feel energetic enough to make a detour, why not try the 'old road' from Rethimnon to Hania (264km) — this route is described on page 32, beginning in the second paragraph.

8 THE AMARI VALLEY

**Hania • Rethimnon • Apostoli • Thronos • Fourfouras
• Agios Ioannis • Gerakari • Rethimnon • Hania**

240km/149mi; 6 hours' driving; Exit A from Hania (see plan page 8)

On route: Picnics (see pages 10-12): (8a, 8b); CT8; Walks 7, 8, (9), 28,
29 (Walks 30 and 31 are nearby)

*The tour follows predominantly reasonable asphalted country roads,
but they are narrow in places.*

The Amari Valley forms a natural route from the north to the south and so was much used as a refuge during the Second World War. Encircled by some forty villages and dotted with Byzantine churches, the valley offers up lovely countryside along our immediate route. But we also enjoy awe-inspiring, sweeping views encompassing the southwest slopes of Psiloritis, Crete's highest peak, and the string of mountains formed by Kedros, Soros, Fortetza and Vrissinas.

Follow the notes for Car tour 7 (page 33) to **Rethimnon**. Go through the first set of traffic lights (59km) and *pass* the turn off to Spili and Amari, which is taken in Car tour 7. Take the *next* turn-off right, following signs for Amari. As you travel towards Prasies, looking southwest, you will see Vrissinas (858m) — the highest peak across the valley and the goal of Walk 9. **Prasies** (71km 🛉) is very pretty and shows signs of its Venetian past. Beyond the village, at the top of a ridge (72km), you enjoy the spectacular view (📷) towards the Prassanos Gorge shown on page 62. Soon, just past the turning right to Mirthios, you pass the starting point for Walk 7, which explores this gorge.

Take care at a narrow bridge (74km), which has to be negotiated before you descend into the valley (80km ✕🍴). Then the road climbs up again, out of the valley, and runs along beside it. **Apostoli** (90km 🛉✕ and 🍴 just beyond the village) is at the head of the Amari Valley. Our circuit will bring you back to this point. Keep straight on through **Agia Fotini** (91km 🍴) and stay on the main road until, on a bend, you see a sign for **Thronos**. It leads you left and up to the village (92km 🛉). After visiting the church, return to the main road and turn left, continuing the circuit. Pass below Kalogeros (🛉 with 14th-century frescoes), a pretty

Agios Ioannis Theologos, near Gerakari (Car tour 8)

35

hillside village set up to the left of the road, and — a minute beyond here — look right to see the small 15th-century Byzantine church of Agia Paraskevi.

Pass the junction (93.5km) to Amari and keep straight on the main road (🚰 97km) as it curves left. Go through **Afratas** (100km) and continue through groves of ancient olive trees, with fine views right towards Amari. Then come into **Visari** (103km). The road curls round the edge of the village and heads up to **Fourfouras** (105km 🚰). Walk 29 (photograph page 125) starts in this village, which is mainly set down to the right of the road. Behind Fourfouras lies Mt Kedros (1777m/5830ft) — a very comfortable mound, compared to the tantalising jagged teeth and high slopes of Psiloritis to the left of the road. Two kilometres past Fourfouras, as you continue to climb, look right and back over the village and the entire basin of the Amari Valley below you (📷).

Drive on via **Kouroutes** (112km 🍴) and **Nithavris** (116km). Here, at the end of the village, turn right (by a war memorial) towards Agios Ioannis. This route cuts across the valley and goes through the upper part of **Agios Ioannis** (120km). Turn *sharp right* at 120.5km for Rethimnon (*don't* head for Agia Paraskevi). The Rethimnon road now takes you through the lower part of Agios Ioannis.

As you cross a bridge (125.5km) over the River Platys look right to see the picturesque old bridge shown on page 10 (Picnic CT8). Past the bridge, the road starts to climb up the west side of the valley, above the olive tree line. Go through **Hordaki** (132km) in a matter of moments and **Ano Meros** (136km) — a somewhat tumbledown, but not unattractive village of red-roofed houses, where Walk 28 starts. There's a striking war memorial at the far end of the village, portraying a woman with a hammer in her hand. Mt Samitos rises to the right of the small village of **Drigies** (138km). Move on through **Vrises** and **Kardaki** and then, just before Gerakari, keep watch on the right for the ruined monastery of Agios Ioannis Theologos (🍴) shown on pages 34-35; it houses Byzantine frescoes dating from the 13th century. Even in the autumn, **Gerakari** (145km) is visibly greener than the rest of the countryside. A cemetery on the left precedes **Meronas** (150km 🍴), where fresh spring water pours down hillsides.

Turn left in **Agia Fotini** (155km), following signposting to Rethimnon. Go straight into **Apostoli**. You have now completed the valley circuit. Once back in **Rethimnon**, join the national road heading west for Hania (240km).

❀ Walking

Western Crete is certainly a walkers' paradise but, even if you aren't an avid walker, there are plenty of opportunities for gentle strolls and rambles in the depths of the countryside, where you will develop a real appreciation for this magnificent corner of Greece. So if you can't 'do Samaria', you *could* manage a good number of our walks in western Crete. And one of the best features of these other walks is that from start to finish you may be alone with the landscape and a few local people … bliss.

The 'Landscapes' series is built around walks and excursions that can be done in day trips from your base. However, it is possible to link a certain number of our walks by spending a night or two away from your hotel — thus making a patchwork of mountain, gorge and coastal paths (see, for instance, Walks 16-26).

There are, of course, many more walks in western Crete than those we have described in this book, but most of them would involve being based in a more out-of-the-way location — or they would be quite far off a bus route. We feel that the walks we have included present an attractive cross-section of land- and seascapes — the real character of western Crete.

Some words of advice: **Never try to get from one walk to another on uncharted terrain.** Only link up walks by following paths described in these notes, or by using roads or tracks. Don't try to cross rough country, unless you are in the company of a local guide — it might be dangerous. **Never** try to cross military installations or to take photographs in the area.

Do greet anyone you pass or see working in a field when you are out walking. The people you meet are very much a part of the landscape, countryside and essence of Crete, and will reciprocate your gesture of friendliness and acknowledgement.

There are walks in this book for everyone:

Beginners: Start on the walks graded 'easy' or 'straight-forward'; good examples are Walks 1, 2, 5, 12, 15, 16, 20 (Short walk), 25 and 31. *You need look no further than the picnic suggestions on pages 10-12 to find a large selection of very easy walks.*

Experienced walkers: If you are accustomed to rough

terrain and are feeling fit, you should be able to manage and enjoy all the walks in this book. Several of them are very long, so your hiking experience will stand you in good stead. Note that a couple of walks will demand that you have a head for heights. Take into account the season and weather conditions. Don't attempt the more strenuous walks in high summer; do protect yourself from the sun and carry ample water and fruit. *Always remember that storm damage could make any walk described in this book unsafe.* Remember, too, always to follow the route as we describe it. If you have not come to one of our landmarks after a reasonable time, you must go back to the last 'sure' point and start again.

Experts: Head for the high mountains. Both the White Mountains and the Ida Range (Psiloritis) will be a great attraction for you (Walks 4, 19, 20, 29, 30).

Guides, waymarking, maps

Experienced walkers, used to taking compass readings, will not need a guide for any walk in this book, but should you wish to go further afield we suggest you contact the Greek Alpine Club (EOS) beneath Olympic Airways on Tsanakaki in Hania, or the refuge at Kallergi above Omalos: Tel 0821-74560. The refuge is managed by Josef Schwemberger, an Austrian, who speaks English.

Many of the routes in the west of the island are **waymarked**, some by daubs of red paint, some by cairns. In addition there is a network of 'E4'-marked routes. These 'European Rambler Trails' are very well waymarked with black and yellow metal flags and paint marks. If a walk in the book has become part of an E4 route, we have identified it and kept the text to a minimum.

The only largish-scale **maps** of Crete are those published by Harms Verlag* (scale 1:80,000). We find this scale too small for walking, however, so we continue to draw up our own routes in the field, based on old 1:50,000 topographical maps which we have updated with new roads. Since no modern 1:50,000 maps are available for reference, it is virtually impossible for us to make our routes *exact* or to show all the new tracks built in the last few years. The notes themselves should enable you to do any walk without problems; we hope the maps will give you a feel for the 'lie of the land'.

*Second edition, 1995/6, published in five sheets and available in the UK from your usual map stockist.

Things that bite or sting

Dogs on Crete, in our experience, are full of bravado, but not vicious. They bark like fury — indeed, what would be the point of guarding livestock if they did not? — and they will approach you, seemingly full of evil intention. However, they will shy off, if you continue unperturbed. 'El-la' is a useful word to know. It means 'come here', if spoken encouragingly, or 'come off it', when said in a slightly diffident tone. Use it encouragingly with the dogs, and they'll soon calm down. If you carry a walking stick, keep it out of sight and don't use it threateningly.

In the autumn you may be startled by **gunfire**, but it's only hunters — invariably on Sundays and holidays — in pursuit of game. You'll doubtless see them dropping or throwing stones into bushes — Greek beating!

Have respect for **donkeys**' hind legs; it's highly unlikely they'll kick, but don't forget the possibility.

Snakes may be seen, and **vipers** have been identified on Crete, but they keep a low profile. Poisonous **spiders**, called *rogalida*, do exist on the island, but it's unlikely you'll glimpse one of these burrowers. You're more likely to see **scorpions**; they are harmless, but their sting is painful. They, like spiders and snakes, are most likely hiding under rocks and logs in the daytime. So if you move a rock etc to sit down, just have a look under it first!

People who are allergic to bee stings should always carry the necessary pills with them. **Bees** abound in high summer, especially around water troughs and thyme bushes. It's also worth taking a plug-in **mosquito** deterrent, mosquito repellent, and some anti-sting ointment.

What to take

If you're already on Crete when you find this book, and you haven't any special equipment such as a rucksack or walking boots, you can still do many of the walks — or you can buy the basic equipment. For each walk in the book, the *minimum* equipment is listed. But it would be a good idea to consider this checklist before setting out:

stout shoes with ankle support or walking boots; (long) socks
waterproof rain gear (outside summer months)
long-sleeved shirt (sun protection)
long trousers, tight at the ankles
water bottle, plastic plates, etc
anorak (zip opening)
whistle, torch, compass

sunhat, sunglasses, suncream
spare bootlaces
insect repellent, antiseptic cream
up-to-date bus timetable
bandages, plasters, tissues
knives and openers
light cardigans (or similar)
small rucksack
plastic groundsheet

Please bear in mind that we've not done every walk in this book under *all* conditions. We do know that you need plenty of water for every walk, but we might not realise, for example, just how hot or how exposed some walks might be. Beware the sun and the effects of dehydration. Don't be deceived by cloud cover: you can still get sunburnt, especially on the back of your neck and legs. *Always* carry a long-sleeved shirt and long trousers to put on when you've had enough sun, and **always wear a sunhat**. Have your lunch in a shady spot on hot days and carry a good supply of water and fruit. In spring and autumn, remember that it might be cold in the mountains. We rely on your good judgement to modify the equipment list at the start of each walk, according to the season.

Where to stay

We have used Hania as our walking base, since the majority of people stay there when visiting western Crete. But we have taken into account those of you staying at Rethimnon, Kastelli, or along the south coast, and you will find that you can join many of the car tours without difficulty. If you wish to do some of the walks, several will be on your doorstep, but check in the bus timetables (pages 133-134) to make sure that the walks furthest from your base are practicable. Due to the size of the island, some of the walks in the west require bus changes. Although this makes the day longer, it has the advantage that you see more of the countryside. To find rooms in small villages, enquire at the local tavernas and cafeneions about renting a bed for a night. An overnight stay at Kallergi is recommended for those of you tackling the Levka Ori (see page 38, 'Guides').

Weather

April, May, September and October are perhaps the best months to walk on Crete. The air temperature is moderate, but the sun shines. It *is* possible to walk during June, July and August, however, because although it may be very hot by the coast, there's often a light breeze in the mountains. There's no doubt it's more tiring though, and great care should be taken in the sun and heat. Walks offering no shade at all (for instance Walk 11 on the Rodopou Peninsula) should *never* be undertaken in high summer.

The *meltemi* blowing in from the north tends to be a bad-tempered wind, bringing strong hot breezes in the height of summer. These breezes stir up the dust, move the air about, but don't really cool it.

During February and November it often rains. The months of December and January are chilly and, if it rains, it may do so for two or three days at a time. However, the winter in Crete brings an incredible clarity on the clear sunny days and some really perfect walking weather, when temperatures may be around 20°C (68°F).

It's worth remarking too that, more often than not, when it's windy along the north coast, it's invariably calm on the south of the island.

Walkers' checklist

The following points cannot be stressed too often:
- **At any time a walk may become unsafe** due to storm damage or road construction. If the route is not as described in this book, and your way ahead is not secure, do *not* attempt to continue.
- **Never walk alone** — four is the best walking group.
- **Do not overestimate your energies**: your speed will be determined by the slowest walker in the group.
- **Transport connections** at the end of a walk are vital.
- **Proper footwear** is essential.
- **Warm clothing** is needed in the mountains; even in summer, take something appropriate with you, in case you are delayed.
- **Compass, torch, whistle** weigh little, but might save your life.
- **Extra food** and drink should be taken on long walks.
- **Always take a sunhat** with you, and in summer a cover-up for your arms and legs as well.
- A **stout stick** is a help on rough terrain.
- **Do not panic** in an emergency.
- Read and re-read the **important note on page 2** and the country code on page 13, as well as guidelines on grade and equipment for each walk you plan to do.

Greek for walkers

In the major tourist centres you hardly need to know any Greek but, once out in the countryside, a few words of the language will be helpful ... and much appreciated.

Here's one way to ask directions in Greek *and understand the answers you get!* First memorise the 'key' questions below. Then, always follow up your key question with **a second question demanding a yes (ne) or no (ochi) answer**. Greeks invariably raise their heads to say 'no', which looks to us like the beginning of a 'yes'. (By the way, 'ochi' (no) might be pronounced as o-heé, o-sheé or even oi-eé.)

Following are the two most likely situations in which you may have to use some Greek. The dots (...) show where you fill in the name of your destination. See Index for the approximate pronunciation of place names.*

■ **Asking the way**

The key questions

English	Approximate Greek pronunciation
Good day, greetings	**Hair**-i-tay
Hello, hi (informal)	**Yas**-sas (plural); **Yia**-soo (singular)
Please — where is	**Sas** pa-ra-ka-**loh** — **pou ee**-nay
the road that goes to ... ?	o **thr**o-mo stoh ... ?
the footpath that goes to ... ?	ee mono-**pati** stoh ... ?
the bus stop?	ee **sta**-ssis?
Many thanks.	Eff-hah-ree-**stoh** po-li.

Secondary questions leading to a yes/no answer

English	Approximate Greek pronunciation
Is it here?/there?	**Ee**-nay etho?/eh-**kee**?
Is it straight ahead?/behind?	**Ee**-nay kat-eff-**thia**?/**pee**-so?
Is it to the right?/left?	**Ee**-nay thex-**ya**?/aris-teh-**rah**?
Is it above?/below?	**Ee**-nay eh-**pano**?/**kah**-to?

■ **Asking a taxi driver to take you somewhere and return for you, or asking a taxi driver to collect you somewhere**

English	Approximate Greek pronunciation
Please —	**Sas** pa-ra-ka-**loh** —
Would you take us to ...?	Tha **pah**-reh mas stoh ...?
Come and pick us up	**El**-la-teh na mas **pah**-reh-teh
from ... (place) at ... (time)	apo ... stis ...

(Instead of memorising the hours of the day, simply point out on your watch the time you wish to be collected.)

As you may well need a taxi for some walks, why not ask your tour rep or hotel receptionist to find a driver who speaks English. We'd also recommend that you use an inexpensive phrase book: they give easily-understood pronunciation hints, as well as a good selection of useful phrases.It's unlikely that a map will mean anything to the people you may meet en route. Doubtless, they will ask you, '**Pooh pah**-tay'? — at the same time turning a hand over in the air, questioningly. It means 'Where are you going?', and quite a good answer is 'Stah voo-**na**', which means 'To the mountains'. (We could insert here a long list of their comments on this, to which you would smile and plough on, 'Landscapes' guide in hand ...)

*Accents are not printed on place names in the text, lest it slow up your reading, however they are shown in the Index and on the maps.

Organisation of the walks

The 31 main walks in this book are located in the parts of western Crete most easily accessible by public transport, using Hania (or Rethimnon) as the base. We hope that even if you are staying at another location in the west, most will be within range. (Although the walking notes show bus departures from Hania, you will find more complete timetables on pages 133-134, including Rethimnon, Kastelli, etc.)

The book is set out so that you can plan walks easily — depending on how far you want to go, your abilities and equipment — and what time you are willing to get up in the morning! You might begin by considering the fold-out touring map between pages 16 and 17. Here you can see at a glance the overall terrain, the road network, and the location of all the walks, which are outlined in white. Quickly flipping through the book, you'll find that there's at least one photograph for each walk.

Having selected one or two potential excursions from the map and the photographs, look over the planning information at the beginning of each walk description. Here you'll find distance/hours, grade, equipment, and how to get there and return. If the walk sounds beyond your ability or fitness, check if there's a shorter or alternative version given. We've tried to provide walking opportunities less demanding of agility wherever possible.

When you are on your walk, you will find that the text begins with an introduction to the overall landscape and then quickly turns to a detailed description of the route itself. Times are given for reaching certain points in the walk. Giving times is always tricky, because they depend on so many factors, but once you've done one walk you'll be able to compare our very steady pace with your own; we hope you'll find we're in step, give or take! Note that our times *do not include any stops*, so allow for them.

The large-scale maps (see notes on page 38: 'Guides, waymarking, maps') have been overprinted to show important landmarks. Below is a key to the symbols:

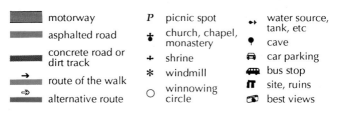

▬▬	motorway	*P*	picnic spot	•→	water source, tank, etc
▬▬	asphalted road	✝	church, chapel, monastery	●	cave
▬▬	concrete road or dirt track	✛	shrine	🚗	car parking
→	route of the walk	✳	windmill	🚌	bus stop
⇒	alternative route	○	winnowing circle	Π	site, ruins
				📷	best views

1 CIRCUIT VIA AGIA

See also photograph page 2   **Distance:** 11km/6.8mi; 3h05min
Grade: straightforward walk on tracks and roads, with about 200m/650ft of ascents overall
Equipment: trainers, sunhat, picnic, water
How to get there and return: any 🚌 calling at Kato Stalos (currently Timetables 5, 6, 7, 8, 9; when the national road is complete, probably only Timetable 9 will cover this route); journey time 10min
Shorter walk: Kato Stalos — Agia (6km/3.7mi; 2h10min). Grade, equipment, access as above. Follow the main walk to Agia and return by Omalos 🚌 (Timetable 3), Sougia 🚌 (Timetable 6), or blue town 🚌.
Short walk: Agia — lake — Agia (1.7km/1mi; 35min). Easy, level walk; equipment as main walk. Access: Omalos 🚌 (Timetable 3), Sougia 🚌 (Timetable 6), or blue town bus to/from Agia. From the main road take the turning 'Kirtomados 2km'. Soon, keep right at a fork. Pass a church on the left, cross a bridge with iron railings, then turn right to the lake.
Alternative walk: Agia — Kato Stalos (6km/3.7mi; 2h). Easy, mostly level walking; access as Short walk; equipment and return as main walk. Follow the Short walk past the lake and, when you get to the shrine of Agios Nektarios, either go left or right (the way to the right is flatter).

The lake at Agia is a particularly good place to watch birds, a lovely quiet oasis overlooked by the church of Saints Constandinos and Eleni — hence the name Agia, which means 'holy'.

Start out by taking the road opposite the Shell petrol station, signposted to Stalos. When the road forks, go right. Some **15min** along you will see a lovely old house on the far side of the valley. Built in the 1700s, it is a classic example of the Turkish style of that era. To its right — beyond its garden, under two or three large trees, you will notice a semi-circular hole in the wall. Water for the household flowed from the mountains all those years ago, through this hole and into a stone pool. The water, having been used for washing clothes — and people — was then allowed to drain into the valley to water the fruit trees.

Beyond the cemetery you pass two tavernas on the left as you enter the old village of Stalos (its church is shown on page 2). In the middle of the village, pass a turning right, opposite a cafeneion, and continue straight ahead. As you leave Stalos, asphalt gives way to rough track and you head on through olive groves. Stay on the main track, ignoring any turnings left or right. The track climbs gently away from the coast, levels out, then starts to descend.

Cross a concrete bridge and then pass the small church of Profitis Ilias up to the left (**1h**). At the junction here, keep on the main route, as it bends down to the right. There is a fine panorama of countryside ahead. Soon you will see a church and graveyard below you. Curl on down past the church and keep on going round to the left.

Some **1h30min** into the walk, you will see your destination down and across to your left. First of all Agia's church comes into view; then you'll see the lake. Round the next bend, the village of Kirtomados comes into range. When you are in line with the first house in Kirtomados, on your right, take a concrete track going down left through the village. In the midst of the village, at a junction of sorts (where there's a large mulberry tree on the left), weave right and then turn left in front of a large old house with an arched wooden door. Five minutes later, turn left onto the road. At the next junction, where there is a shrine dedicated to Agios Nektarios, follow the road round to the right (the rough track straight ahead is the return route).

Some **1h45min** en route, just before a bridge, take a track going left. In two minutes you will be at the edge of the lake. There is an old stone shelter from which to

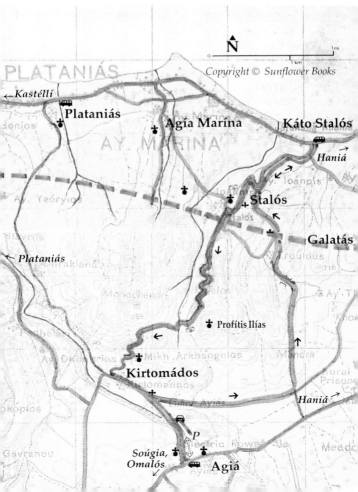

Copyright © Sunflower Books

The grassy banks at Agia's lake (Picnic 1), a fine spot for bird-watchers

birdwatch, or go right and find a place to edge through the reeds. Look out for turtles, too, basking on the rocks.

If you are doing the Shorter walk, from here head back to the road, go left and continue to the main Hania road at Agia; both the blue city buses and the country buses stop opposite the end of this road from Kirtomados.

For the main walk, retrace your steps to the Agios Nektarios shrine on the bend outside Kirtomados and turn right on the rough track; it soon becomes asphalted. In 20 minutes you pass a night club (probably well-sited, assuming the birds enjoy the vibration); overhead wires cross the road here. Ignore the next track going off left but, two minutes past the club/disco, turn left where a track crosses the road. Six minutes later ignore a track on the left and shortly afterwards, when the track forks, keep left. After a while the track starts to go gently downhill.

Stay on the main track and within 20 minutes (45min from Agia) you will see two eucalyptus trees and then another two, on the left. Here a track goes off right: ignore it and continue downhill. Two minutes later, at a T-junction, turn left and cross a small concrete bridge. Follow the track gently up the side of the valley, then bear right on an asphalt road (1h from Agia; **2h50min**). At the next T-junction turn left, leaving a shrine on the corner. In a couple of minutes the roofs of Metochi will be just below you on the left, the old Turkish house first seen as you climbed to Stalos. Fifteen minutes later you will be back on the main road at Kato Stalos (**3h05min**) — having crossed over or under the new national road from Hania to Kastelli, under construction at press date.

2 THERISO • ZOURVA • MESKLA • LAKKI

See photograph pages 24-25   **Distance:** 10.5km/6.5mi; 3h40min

Grade: straightforward, mainly on a track; approximately 400m/1300ft of ascent overall, and 550m/1800ft of descent

Equipment: stout shoes, sunhat, picnic, water

How to get there: 🚌 to Theriso (not in the timetables, but departs Hania 07.30 in season; enquire locally); journey time 30min
To return: 🚌 from Meskla 07.30,14.30 or Lakki 07.00,14.30 (not in the timetables). During high season there are more buses going through Lakki, from Omalos, from Monday to Saturday.

Shorter walk: Theriso — Zourva — Meskla (8km/5mi; 2h10min). Grade, equipment, access as main walk (but you avoid about 200m/650ft of ascent to Lakki). Follow the main walk to Meskla and catch a 🚌 back to Hania (not in the timetables, but departs 14.00 in season; enquire locally); journey time 30min. Alternatively, follow the road (4km/2.5mi; 1h of level walking) from Meskla to Fournes, where you can pick up one of the Hania town buses (no timetables, but they are frequent).

Alternative walk: Drakonas — Theriso (7km/4.3mi; 2h). Grade, equipment as main walk (but the overall ascent is only 250m/800ft). Access: Keramia 🚌 to Drakonas (not in the timetables, but departs 06.00, 14.00); journey time 1h. *(Make sure you take the Keramia bus, because there is another Drakonas near Kastelli.)* To return: 🚗 private transport from Theriso; either ring for a taxi when you get there, or ask friends or a pre-arranged taxi to collect you at the ΑΡΤΕΜΙΟΥ ΠΑΠΑΔΑΚΗ cafeneion. See notes page 49.

Note: It would have been nice to make this a circular walk, but the people whose animals graze in this area have blocked off the route from Meskla up to Theriso, to prevent walkers using it: we have been asked to make it clear that the local people prefer you not to walk here.

Here's a leisurely ramble providing a lovely introduction to the region. The ride from Hania to the start of the walk takes you up via a high-sided gorge lined with plane trees and Spanish chestnuts, to the pretty village of Theriso. Wild flowers cover the hillsides in spring with an almost uncountable variety of blooms. Plan to take a break in Zourva: the taverna alone is worth the walk!

The bus turns round beyond two cafeneions, in front of an old church in Theriso. **Start out** by taking the concrete track heading off to the right of the church (as you face it). The concrete doesn't last for long, as the track climbs away from the village. A streambed is on the left. After about **5min** of gentle climbing, at a hairpin bend signposted right for Zourva, keep left downhill on the main track. You approach a bridge (**10min**), where the main track curves left to Drakonas (the Alternative walk comes in here). Leave the track and take the footpath straight ahead (there may be a netting stock control fence across the path; if so, secure it behind you). Soon you may have to negotiate another stock control fence with oleander beside it. The narrow path (Picnic 2) heads up

47

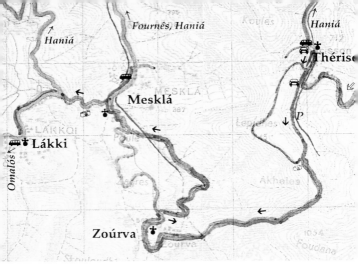

slightly and continues across the hillside, rising away from the tree-lined watercourse.

In **35min** the path divides, just beyond another clump of oleander. Keep to the upper path; it soon heads away from the valley. Five minutes later you'll see some mesh-fenced terraces up ahead. Follow the path to the right of the terracing and head up onto the track above. At the top go straight ahead on the main track, ignoring forks to the left and right. You will see Lakki, with its prominent church, straight ahead in the distance (photograph pages 24-25). Within moments Zourva comes into view, to the left. The track takes you into this village (**1h20min**), where there is a simple but 'special' taverna set up on the right — an ideal place for a sustaining brunch of Aimilia's home-made cheese, bread, honey, eggs, salad and mountain tea. Back on the road, pass the church on the right, and you've left the village in a few minutes.

Follow the asphalt road from Zourva for about 15 minutes; then, after the first *hairpin* bend, turn onto a track leading downhill and back to the right. After two minutes keep left at a first fork. Very shortly go left downhill; then go left again. When the track next forks, stay on the main route, going round to the right (the left fork also leads to Meskla, but the right fork follows the riverbed). At the next fork keep left and downhill. Ten minutes later pass a shrine on the left; at next the two forks you encounter, keep left downhill. Coming within sight of Meskla, 20 minutes from the shrine, the riverbed will be down to the left and you will see the dome of the large village church. Five minutes later, at the following T-junction, turn hard

Copyright © Sunflower Books

left (a right would bring you to the far end of the village). There is a goathouse on the next big bend, where the route crosses the plane tree-lined streambed. The track rises up left from the stream to meet an asphalt road on a bend: go right downhill to the church (**2h10min**). Nearby is a taverna and running water. *To end the Shorter walk,* cross the main village bridge to find the bus stop outside a cafeneion — or continue by road to Fournes (1h).

To make for Lakki, turn left on a track just *before* the bridge (there is a large telegraph pole on the corner). Pass by someone's back yard, with chickens and wood piles, and start climbing — first on concrete, then on rough track. Keep up right at the bend where you can see a church off to the left. At the next fork (five minutes from Meskla), keep right, following signposting to Lakki. Keep to the main track all the way, climbing past any turn-offs left or right. Half an hour from Meskla there is another nice view back over the village and the hills beyond it. An hour from Meskla, join the main road and turn left to Lakki (**3h40min**). The bus leaves from the main square.

Alternative walk (Drakonas — Theriso)

This easy country walk is pleasant in its own right, but, for those of you with plenty of stamina, why not tack it on to the start of the main walk? The bus stops in front of the church at Drakonas. Start out by walking to the left of the church — onto a track (asphalted for the first 200m/yds). The track forks almost immediately: keep right. At the next fork go round to the left (the main track). *Always keep to the main track:* after 1km, at some houses, it curves left. Some 30min from Drakonas keep left at a fork. By 50min there is a splendid mountain view over to the right; the peaks will be with you from now on. As you reach the top of the climb (1h), notice two shrines up on the right, where the track divides. Go straight ahead; there are terraced vines down to the left. At the next fork (where a small sign in Greek indicates Theriso to the left and Drakonas right), bend hard left, down towards the vineyards. At 1h15min ignore a turning right. When there are pine trees either side of your route, ignore a small track going downhill to the left. Eight minutes later keep straight ahead, where a track goes back off the main one. Now (1h30min) you can see Theriso ahead. The track bends away from the village, then back towards it. Beyond a watercourse, look carefully for a netting fence and a footpath going left uphill, into the undergrowth. (Take this path if you are continuing to Meskla or Lakki — follow the main walk from the 10min-point.) Five minutes later, the track forks: keep right downhill. A very old church, set below on the right, heralds the beginning of Theriso and is where the bus turns round. There are two cafeneions here, both on the right, where a taxi could meet you. The one furthest beyond the church is ΑΡΤΕΜΙΟΥ ΠΑΠΑΔΑΚΗ.

3 FROM KATOHORI TO STILOS (OR NIO HORIO)

See map pages 54-55

Distance: 9km/5.6mi; 3h35min to Stilos (4h to Nio Horio)

Grade: moderate to difficult; waymarked gorge walk descending about 200m/650ft; clambering necessary in places

Equipment: stout shoes or boots, sunhat, picnic, water

How to get there: Kambi 🚌 to Katohori (not in the timetables, but departs Hania 06.00 in season; enquire locally); journey time 35min
To return: 🚌 from Stilos (not in the timetables; departs 16.45 in season; enquire locally); journey time 30min, or 🚌 from Nio Horio (not in the timetables; departs 11.15, 13.10, 17.30 weekdays, 11.15, 16.20, 18.30 Saturdays/Sundays in season; enquire locally); journey time 30min

This is a pleasant, but somewhat taxing walk through glorious gorge country. The bus ride from Hania is very well worth the early morning start. The White Mountains rise in an awesome but splendid mass to one side of the route as you climb into the foothills. The gorge itself is an attractive walking route, fringed with leafy plane trees and hemmed with pretty pink oleander bushes near the end of the walk. In parts the walk is demanding, as the gorge floor offers every kind of surface underfoot.

The bus stops just before a bridge where the road curves right (signposted in Greek to Kambi). **To start the walk,** cross the road and walk straight on along a road signposted 'Xania (Hania) 21km'. The riverbed that runs through the gorge to Stilos is down to your right. On the first big U bend to the left, where there is a miniature concrete church, leave the road and carry straight on along the concrete track. The route forks: go right and walk past a small old church on the right. Four minutes later pass another, large church on the left. Go on into a small square, past a huge telephone pole on the left and a cafeneion on the right. Just before the cafeneion, take the track leading off *slightly* left; ignore the full left turn. The route makes for a very distinct knob of rock you will notice pointing skyward in the middle distance ahead.

The track, which leads through orange groves, is likely to be wet, particularly in spring. Anywhere around here is a delightful picnic setting (Picnic 3a). Turn left (**15min**); there may be a cairn marking the start of the route, and soon you will see blue paint waymarks indicating your direction. There are also red dot waymarks along the way. When the track meets the riverbed, cross it. Then, when it comes to the edge of another watercourse, cross to the bank on the far side, then take the footpath ahead, rather than the one going right. You will be led along the edge of the watercourse (Picnic 3b); make your way along

50

beside it — negotiating a fence, if you encounter one. In less than **1h** the landscape opens out somewhat; then the towering sides of the gorge close in on us again.

At **2h30min** you will have to clamber carefully over some rocks; take your time. After **2h50min** you will notice the gorge coming to an end, as the countryside opens out. The walk continues in and beside the riverbed. But at **3h05min** the waymarking leads us up to the right, away from the oleander-lined riverbed and onto an earthen track. Within three to four minutes keep straight on, where a track goes off right. A minute further on the track divides; go straight on, on the right-hand side of the riverbed. Five minutes later the track goes back into the riverbed for 50m/yds, then heads up left, to a bridge on the main road.

Once on the main road, turn right over the bridge, pass a shrine to St Pantelimon and continue into Stilos (**3h35min**), where there are two bus stops. One is opposite the large shady open area, outside a cafeneion; the other is a little further on, opposite the Neo Demokratia head-quarters, marked with a blue and white sign. Rather than wait for the late afternoon bus, why not walk to Nio Horio just 25 minutes away? Here you can pick up one of the more frequent buses or a taxi. The bus stops opposite the kiosk which you will see as you approach the village.

On a hot day the leafy depths of this pretty inland gorge near Katohori provide welcome shade (Picnic 3b).

4 KAMBI • VOLIKA REFUGE • KAMBI

Distance: 14km/8.7mi; 4h55min

Grade: very strenuous, with an ascent/descent of some 700m/2300ft

Equipment: walking boots, long trousers, long socks, anorak, sunhat, compass, picnic, water

How to get there and return: 🚌 or 🚐 to/from Kambi (not in the timetables, but departs Hania 06.00 and Kambi 14.45 in season; enquire locally); journey time 40min

If you have come to Crete prepared to spend some nights away from your base, consider staying in Kambi the night before starting this hike. It's a very pleasant, quiet village with a relaxed atmosphere. There is a bus up to Kambi at crack of dawn, but as this trek is a real energy-tester, you might find it helpful to be on the spot in the early morning ... particularly if you fancy turning it into an expedition.* As the success of this walk relies on compass readings, do choose a clear day, when the mountains are easily visible and the views are sure to be good.

The bus stops in the village square, by the church. **Set off:** walk right, past the church, on an asphalt road. (The bus continues in the same direction en route for Madaro.) A cafeneion called 'ΗΠΡΟΟΔΟΣ' is straight ahead of you. Walk to the right of it; it is a meeting place for the village elders and a nice place to rest and wait for the Hania bus on your return. Take a compass reading on the corner by the cafeneion, as you pass it. Face the mountains towards which you are heading, which are due south, and notice, in particular, the tree-covered slopes of the ravine shown above opposite. Then continue on the road, disregarding a track to the left passed a few minutes later. Beyond a shrine on the right, come to very pretty, lush countryside; this is a fine picnic spot (Picnic 4). Masses of wildflowers line the route, and it is surrounded by fig trees, walnut trees, vines and olives. Pass another cafeneion that has rows of potted plants and flowers along its length, and a shrine — both on the right. Directly afterwards, at a junction, fork right towards ΠΛΑΤΥΒΟΛΑ (ΜΑΔΑΡΟ is signposted to the left). Very soon your way becomes a dirt track.

Soon after forking right, look up to the spread of mountains again and take note once more of the dark V of the tree-lined ravine, almost in the centre of the view ahead. Turn left at the crossing (**10min**), and then turn right just

*You could hire a guide in Kambi to show you the area *beyond* the EOS hut at Volika, which is our point of return. You would stay overnight at the hut (taking your own provisions), which is otherwise locked. Arrange it via the EOS office beneath Olympic Airways in Hania (Tel: 0821-47647) or at the cafeneion in Kambi run by Georgios Nikilioudakis.

52

Our goal, the Volika refuge, is in the centre of the photograph, just above the tree line.

before the houses. Ignore a path off to the right; keep on the track. When the track runs out in front of a concrete farm building (**25min**) and two footpaths lead off, turn left up the hill. There are three waymark arrows along the first stages of the path, but they soon run out, and you must make your way up the hillside, taking any one of several possible paths. Keep near the fence on your left until, as you draw level with a line of low bumpy hills on your left in the distance, the path heads away from the fence slightly. Continue onwards and upwards, remembering the direction in which you are heading. Keep to the right-hand side along a fence going up the hillside, go through a stock control gate, and continue uphill. Look ahead and get your bearings: there is one prominent, domed mountain in the distance. Between you and it is a hill which is high on the left and low on the right. Directly to your right, the hillside shows signs of track running along it, just below the top. The fence is still 15-20m/yds away on your left. Up to the right, close to the peak of the hill you are climbing, another track can be seen. Climb steeply up to join this track (**45min**). Turn round here and get your bearings for the return. *This is important.* Beyond Souda Bay, in the distance, the Akrotiri (airport) mast is visible. At the left end of the same peninsula, where the mountainside seems to fall into the sea, is Stavros (shown in the photograph on page 25). Further left, pick out the island of Theodorou, just off the north coast at Platanias and, beyond that, the Rodopou Peninsula. *Then take note of Kambi's position very carefully.* These precautions are to save you wading through thistles and thorny burnet on your way back down to the village. Now follow the track uphill.

Further on into the climb up this first hillside (**50min**), when there are more folds of mountains visible ahead, pause to take stock yet again and identify your destination

53

and route. The large domed mountain ahead has trees down the left side of its top. Two 'bumps' from that one, to the left, find a mountain with trees all over its summit. Make for this latter. There are huge bare mountains beyond and to the left of it.

As you come to the top of a rise, the track ends and you find the ruins of a small stone hut. Identify the route to the refuge, which is via the V-shaped ravine, with trees down both its sloping sides. (Before you reach the ravine, and the final climb to the refuge, there is a small gulley to be negotiated.) There *is* waymarking, but it is more directional than an indication of an actual path and, as several people have had a 'go' at waymarking, it's best to just keep your goal in sight and think where you are heading.

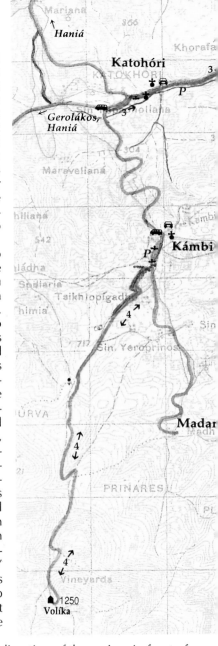

So set off in the direction of the ravine. In front of you, in the distance, there are two trees along your line of sight — one about 20m/yds away, the second about 50m away. There is a small stone hut just beside the second tree, but

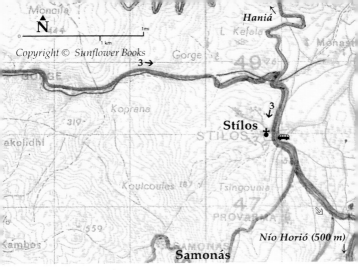

it is barely visible from this point. Some 15m to the left of the second tree, another tree (a wild almond) is prominent. Head towards the first tree, then between the other two. These trees are good landmarks, especially on your return. Stand under one for a moment (**1h**) and look up the ravine. Sharp eyes will be able to pick out the refuge hut, beyond the tree line. Now is the time to decide if you want to go all the way, because it's going to get steep!

Follow the sporadic, directional waymarking towards the ravine; at **1h10min** you will be at the edge of a small wooded gulley. You can see the path going up the far side of it, leading on to the ravine and the climb to Volika. At the bottom of the gulley there is a stone bench with a marble plaque dating from 1982 above it: the Greek inscription ΣΤΑΣΗ ΑΝΤΩΝΗ ΓΑΜΠΑ ΟΡΕΙΒΑΤΙΚΟΣ ΧΑΝΙΟΝ means 'Antonis Gambas Rest Area — Hania Mountaineering Club'. Seven to eight minutes later, having crossed the gulley and taken a breather, cross the flat area beyond. (There are waymarks just above eye level on rocks about 15m/yds apart, either side of the route.)

At **1h30min**, having negotiated some sharp, pale grey rock, you look up the ravine and towards the final ascent. Good waymarking now leads you up the very steep right-hand side of the ravine. Trees provide shade and resting places. After climbing for 20 minutes or so, the path leads you to the other (left) side of the ravine (**1h50min**). Ten minutes later it crosses back to the right. Some 35 minutes from starting up the ravine (**2h25min**), come to a flat wooded area: the ravine appears to end here, but follow the waymarking uphill. The ravine becomes a gulley, wedged in beside layered rock to the left of the route.

Just under an hour from the start of the final ascent the Volika hut comes into sight. Five minutes later the path crosses the gulley on the layered rock. The waymarking is very sparse over this last stretch but, looking at your destination, approach it from the left to find easiest access. By **3h10min** you have the satisfaction of reaching the hut.

The return journey should take much less time, although a large proportion of it requires careful walking and close attention to direction. It will take about an hour to get to the bottom of the ravine. Make your way back and, when you reach the top of the small, wooded gulley on the far side of the ravine, head due north — not northeast. Be sure to go far enough in a northerly direction before turning towards Kambi; wait until you can actually see the village and route on which you started the climb, before heading down towards it, arriving in **4h55min**.

5 GEORGIOUPOLI CIRCUIT

See photographs opposite and pages 29, 61
Distance: 14km/8.7mi; 4h15min
Grade: straightforward climb/descent of 350m/1150ft, but with some overgrown paths to negotiate
Equipment: stout shoes, sunhat, picnic, water, swimming things, long trousers/socks
How to get there and return: 🚌 or any Rethimnon or Iraklion 🚌 (Timetables 1, 2) to/from Georgioupoli; journey time 45min
Shorter walk: Circuit from Argirimouri (8km/5mi; 2h45min). Grade, equipment as main walk. Access by 🚌 car; park near Georgia's Taverna in Argirimouri and pick up the walk at the 45min-point.

Georgioupoli is a pleasant place, not only for walking, but for eating, swimming and just relaxing. This walk gives you a lovely countryside contrast to the busier coast. At the end of this walk, it's worth crossing the national road to the lake at Kournas (where Walk 6 ends) — for a fresh-water swim or quiet lakeside taverna meal.

Start out at the bus stop on the national road, opposite the Georgioupoli turn-off. Cross the road and walk to the village square. Follow the road straight across the square and down over a bridge which spans the fishing harbour (photograph page 61). There's a lovely view out to sea on your right and up to the mountains on your left. Walk away from the village, passing taverna signs right and left. Some **10min** from the square, ignore a track off right, then another a few minutes later, and finally a third rough track (where there is a mulberry and a pine tree set back from the road). Take the *next* track to the right: it leaves the main road on a bend. Climb past some tall conifers; you meet the road again in a couple of minutes and follow it uphill. On the next big bend in the road, climb a steep narrow footpath up to the right. Halfway up the rise, turn right on a well-established, wide stony footpath. When it forks, go left; in a couple of minutes you emerge in front of Georgia's Taverna at Argirimouri; it's to the right of the main road (**45min**). Walk to the right, passing the front of the taverna, and then take a track off to the left, just beside the taverna. Look for waymarking which starts along here.

Some **50min** into the walk, after a concreted section, look up and you will see the way to Likotinara indicated ahead — a footpath off to the left, just beyond the gate to a house. Keep looking for cairns and occasional red waymarks as the path heads north/northeast up the hillside. Half way up the hillside, a wall starts on the right hand side of the path and, as you are nearing the top, the path

Left: View to the White Mountains, 1h10min above Georgioupoli

passes an old walled-in well on the right.

At **1h25min** the path rises up to a track, where you go left. After a few minutes the roofs of Likotinara come into view, and the sea is seen to the right. Some 10-15 minutes later take an old cobbled path going off to the right (marked by a cairn) and head down towards Likotinara. (If the path is very overgrown in spring, continue on the track into the village.) Eight minutes on the cobbled path brings you into the village, where you meet asphalt. Turn right and walk to the viewpoint over the coast and distant mountains. There is a monument here to the Communist Resistance fighters.

Returning from the viewpoint, come to a fork in the road: go left towards Litsarda (signposted in Greek; Kefalas is to the right). Pass a sign indicating you are leaving Likotinara and, eight minutes later (**2h05min**), walk past the sign at the start of Selia and go on into the village. Three minutes into it, at a junction, follow the road in a bend to the right. After about 200m/yds, opposite a playground/basket-ball area, take the track going off left (by a shrine at the corner of a house). Very soon the track becomes a cobbled path, heading south. Within five minutes you will see that the path runs above and parallel with the road. If you are walking in spring and the undergrowth is too

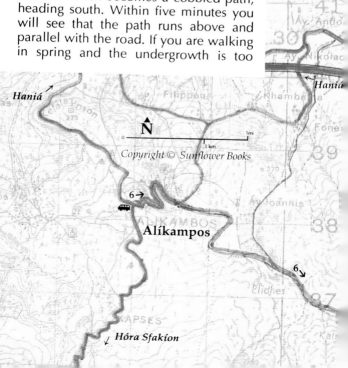

dense, you could join the road here. Some **2h20min** into the walk, you will see the sea again at Georgioupoli. Follow the waymarking; 20 minutes from Selia the path broadens out, by a stone wall bending right, down to the road. If necessary, move or lift a thorn barrier and continue on the path (there is a cairn ahead). Then join the road and head left downhill. At a right-hand bend, in line with the first houses of Kali Amigdali, you can take a short-cut path down to the left. When you meet the road again, at a junction (**3h**), go straight across and 10 minutes later walk into Exopolis.

Follow the narrow road up to the left and, when it forks, keep straight ahead. Pass a church on your right. Curve right at the next junction and almost immediately you will see Georgioupoli down to the right. Follow the narrow road down to Georgia's Taverna *(the Shorter walk ends here)*. Now retrace your steps to the bridge and walk back through the village, arriving at the road and bus stop 10 minutes later (**4h15min**).

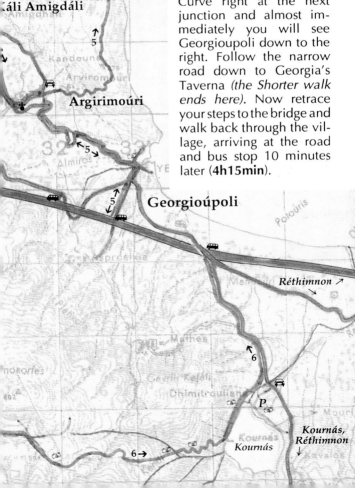

6 ALIKAMPOS • KOURNAS LAKE • GEORGIOUPOLI

See map pages 58-59; see also photograph page 29

Distance: 13km/8mi; 4h30min

Grade: moderate to strenuous; an easy climb of 200m/650ft on a track, then a steep descent of 500m/1650ft on a footpath. You must be sure-footed and agile. Take care near the lake if the shepherds' dogs are guarding the sheep-fold, although they are *usually* tied up.

Equipment: stout shoes, sunhat, picnic, water, swimming things

How to get there: Hora Sfakion 🚌 to the Alikampos turn-off, 7km south of Vrises (Timetable 4); journey time 45min
To return: 🚌 from Georgioupoli (Timetables 1, 2); journey time 50min

As soon as you feel ready for a testing walk, try this one. It combines straightforward walking in pleasant countryside with a good measure of downhill scrambling in a dry ravine. The lake at Kournas is the only fresh-water lake on Crete, and it makes an attractive goal.

Start out at the signposted turn-off to Alikampos; follow the tarred road, keeping left at a fork. You come into a small square in Alikampos. There is a war memorial on the right and a cafeneion beyond it, straight ahead. Turn right in front of the cafeneion and start walking away from the village, passing a shrine on the right, then a minor road off to the right. Ignore a road off to the left, then pass a shrine on the left. Now on rough track, ignore another turning off to the left. By **40min** Alikampos is well below you, as you head for the hills along a flower-lined track.

Having passed via Dafnokorfes (the hill on the left; 692m) and Halara (1968m; slightly further off to the right), at **1h35min**, just before the top of the pass, you come to a a crossing track: turn right. Five minutes later this track peters out, just beyond a shepherds' dwelling. Take the footpath to the left of two olive-tree trunks: it strikes out in an east-southeasterly direction. Within four or five minutes the north coast will be spread out in the distance below, off to the left. The path heads downhill beneath a pear tree; keep left where it forks and walk towards the coast. Tread carefully; the path is very steep and you may well find it necessary to scramble. At the bottom, head to the right of the obvious hillock in front of you; then go slightly left downhill, soon turning directly towards the sea.

The path passes an animal stockade on the left (**2h 20min**). Head towards the paddock below on the right. Cross the paddock and continue on out the far side, following the footpath, which soon heads downhill again — it's rough, but well waymarked. It leads under and round a huge olive tree. Beyond the tree there is an open flat area. Walk along its right-hand edge. Once across the flat, the path descends dramatically and needs careful negotiation. This is where the *real* scrambling starts.

Suddenly the lovely green and turquoise lake at Kournas comes into sight, and there are some good places to perch and take in the tremendous view. The route leads across the left side of the ravine. Go under a spreading fig; then make for a huge curving carob. From here, continue down to the dry streambed. *Watch your step.* At **3h 05min** a more discernible footpath leads away from the ravine, but it is only one of several paths through the shrubs. As long as you head towards the lake you can't go wrong, but an obvious route leads via a couple of shepherds' buildings and a sheepfold, and from there to the lake. It divides just beyond the sheepfold; go right. On reaching the lake (1h20min from passing the shepherds' dwelling at the start of the path), go left on the track that hems its perimeter (Picnic 6). It's lovely to swim in this clear water.

At the end of the lake (**3h40min**) the track bends round beside a building on your right. If there is a fence here, get onto the right-hand side of it. Follow the track to the road, 10 minutes away. Turn left along the road until you see a sign indicating Rethimnon right and Hania left. Turn left and cross the bridge over the highway. You are on the old road. You can catch a bus nearby on the highway (**4h30min**), or walk on 2km into Georgioupoli.

Fishing boats at Georgioupoli, bringing in their catch to the tavernas. Early morning is a good time to see them.

7 THE PRASSANOS GORGE

Distance: 11km/6.8mi; 3h30min-5h

Grade: moderate, but agility is required in a couple of places. The overall descent is 300m/1000ft. *Important note:* Outside summer, if there has been heavy rainfall, *the gorge is **not** passable.*

Equipment: stout shoes, sunhat, picnic, water

How to get there: any Rethimnon or Iraklion 🚌 (Timetables 1, 2) to the Rethimnon bus station; journey time 1h. Then take either a 🚕 taxi or an Amari 🚌 (not in the timetables, but departs 07.00,14.00); journey time 30min. Ask for 'Prassanos' (the gorge) or Mirthios.
To return: town 🚌 from Missiria (every 15min); journey time 30min

This gorge is an awe-inspiring and inviting sight as it carves a swathe through the countryside to the coast by Rethimnon. It has obviously been created by great force — as you'll see from the massive boulders en route. The landscape around is very open and pleasing to look at, making a good, accessible walk.

The taxi or bus will drop you at a road junction where a sign indicates Mirthios off to the right. From this junction, **start out** by walking about 100m/yds in the direction of Amari along the road. Then turn left on a concrete track. Immediately you are facing the huge entrance to the gorge; the landscape is tremendous here, open and grand. Just before the concrete runs out, in 50m/yds or so, open the wire gate and go through. When the now-rough track forks, continue straight ahead on the main track, bending downhill through acres of ferns. Some **12min** from the start you will see a farm building. Pass to the left of it. Then pass another breeze-block building to the right and continue downhill, on a track which runs under telephone

Particularly well sited if you're staying in Rethimnon, Prassanos — another of Crete's spectacular gorges — offers a dramatic-looking invitation. This photograph was taken from the top of a ridge not far beyond Prasies (Car tour 8).

wires and loops down towards a watercourse. When the track forks (**15min**), you can go either way, but we prefer the left-hand branch — it's more scenic.

In a minute you come to the streambed: cross it, and then cross over another, larger, streambed lined with plane trees. Follow the track round to the right and emerge into a more open area. The tree-lined streambed is now on your right and ahead, in the middle distance, is a separate cluster of trees just to the left of the tree-lined streambed. Aim for this cluster of trees, following the slightly overgrown but obvious track which leads to it.

Some 100m/yds beyond the cluster of trees there is an E4 sign and orange waymarking along the track. A second E4 sign a little further on shows you where to scramble down a bank towards the riverbed, passing ferns and plane trees and more E4 signs. At the bottom of the steep bank, veer left towards the riverbed — the beginning of the gorge. Some 20m beyond another E4 sign you will see a large concrete cylinder with waymarking in the middle of the riverbed. Continue straight on from here, following the riverbed. *There are no more E4 signs en route.*

Some **33min** into the walk, a wall of the gorge rears up dramatically on your left. At **40min** the riverbed swings left (northwest), and proceeds amongst smooth white boulders. Fantastic rock faces are now all round. When you are confronted with a huge rock face ahead, the riverbed swings 90° to the left, and you encounter some really big boulders, two of which form a kind of opening through which you pass. There may well be birds of prey hovering overhead here. Before long (**48min**) the gorge looks impassable: a 2.5m/8ft drop is in front of you. To avoid it, retrace your steps until you find an easy scramble up the right-hand side of the gorge. Scramble up about 20m/yds and look for a goat trail marked by cairns. Follow the trail for 100m/yds or so, until it eventually meets the riverbed further on. This detour takes about 15 minutes. Now just enjoy the splendour of the gorge; unless there has been recent storm damage, there aren't any more sections as awkward as the one just avoided — although there are a few more climbs/drops from boulder to boulder before the way eases out.

The gorge narrows (**1h20min**), and the streambed is gravelly underfoot. You reach the last narrow pass where the gorge is no more than 3m/12ft wide (**1h50min**). Fifteen minutes later you will be beyond the main part of the gorge, but still on the riverbed.

At **2h30min** there is a grove of young olive trees fenced with wire mesh to the left of the riverbed. Just beyond this grove, a wire and wooden picket fence blocks the riverbed. It is probably a stock control fence, and it is easily climbed. As soon as the wire fencing surrounding the olive grove peters out, climb up to the old olive grove next to it (to the left of the riverbed).

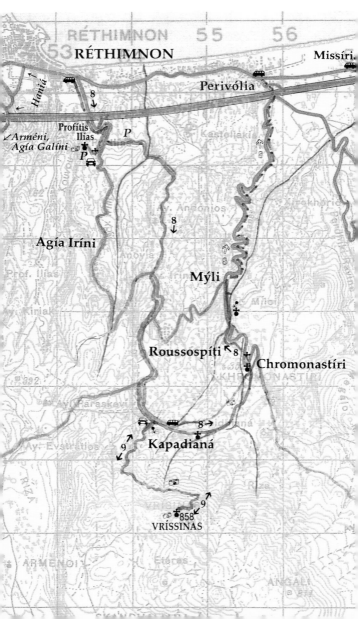

Continue walking in the grove, parallel with the riverbed, until you come across a track one or two trees in from the bank. Follow this track as it turns sharply left, then right, meandering through the old olive grove. Eventually you come to a rusting junkyard — mostly old cars and bedsprings. Continue following the track north towards the sea. You pass an earthen hut used to make charcoal on the left (**3h**). The riverbed, which is nearby on the right, becomes somewhat unattractive, but you can soon see the sea beyond it. You'll see a lovely gently-arching bridge spanning the riverbed (**3h05min**).

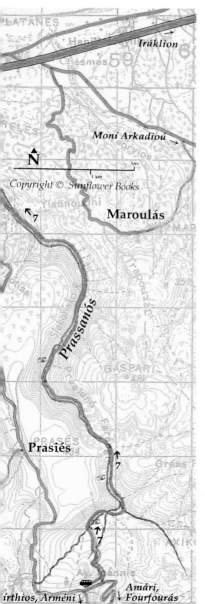

Turn right onto a concrete road which soon acquires an asphalt surface. Continue past some apartments on the left and a cement works on the right. (Well, there are views and there are views!) Walk under the national road and then meet the old main road to Rethimnon in the village of Missiria. Turn left on the road: 150m/yds along, on the right-hand side of the road, there is a bus stop and a public phone box, as well as cafes and tavernas. The bus stop is beyond the sign for Missiria (**3h30min**). Alternatively, you can hail a taxi on this road.

8 RETHIMNON • KAPADIANA • CHROMO-
NASTIRI • MYLI • (PERIVOLIA)

See map pages 64-65

Distance: 11km/6.8mi; 3h50min to Myli (5h15min to Perivolia)

Grade: moderate, with an ascent of under 350m/1150ft

Equipment: stout shoes, sunhat, long socks, picnic, water

How to get there: any Rethimnon or Iraklion 🚌 to Rethimnon bus station and back (Timetables 1, 2); journey time 1 hour; then 🚕 taxi or 🚌 town bus to the kiosk at the corner of Theotokopoulou Street on the eastern outskirts of town, where the walk starts.
To return: 🚕 taxi from Myli (telephone for one on arrival), or walk down to the coastal road at Perivolia to catch a city 🚌 (add 1h15min)

From the busy harbour town of Rethimnon we climb up into the countryside, where we find two old villages well off the beaten track. Then we go on to Myli, where water has taken over from people, leaving the village dramatically deserted — bar one or two stalwarts.

Start out on the outskirts of Rethimnon, at Theotoko-poulou Street, where there is a kiosk set up off the road, on the corner. You won't see the street sign until you are

Over-looking the old, deserted part of Myli

past the kiosk. Walk straight on up the hill, ignoring turnings left and right. You'll soon see the small church of Profitis Ilias perched on a hill. Some **15min** from where you turned off the main road, there is a house on a wide bend in the road. Walk just to the right of the house on a bit of rough track — it cuts a bend off your ascent. Arriving on the road again, by a shrine, take the track off right to the church. This is a lovely picnic setting (Picnic 8a), from where you'll have a splendid view over Rethimnon.

When you're ready to move on, go back down to the road, turn left and, within 80m/yds, take a concrete and stone track that veers off and up to the right of the road. Before long the concrete ends, and rough track is underfoot. There is a fresh-smelling pine wood on your left (Picnic 8b). Ignore the track going off left and other trails through the pines; keep straight on. Soon the way levels out. Every pace immerses you further in the countryside. Some 10 minutes from the road, ignore a turning left and keep walking through olive groves and vineyards. A minute later, where a well-concreted track leads up right and a rough track goes left just ahead of you, keep straight ahead on the main track. Shortly after this 'crossroads', it looks as if your track runs out, but it goes steeply downhill and narrows to footpath for a few metres/yards, where it crosses a watercourse and goes up the other side, soon passing some fig trees.

Meet a T-junction (**50min**) with a concreted track and turn right. A good deal of building is going on around here, on the outskirts of Agia Irini. Walk into and through the village, **1h10min** into the walk. On the far side of the village, you come to a tarmac road; turn left downhill. You will become aware of a church perched far up on the top of Vrissinas, the mountain in the distance. It is a Minoan peak sanctuary — and our goal on Walk 9. Some **1h20min** en route, take the concreted road which forks right and is signposted in Greek 'Καπαδιανα 2km'. The turning is just before the village of Roussospiti. In five minutes, beyond a major bend, the concreted road forks: stay left and then go left again on what has become tarmac road. Ignore tracks off to various building works.

As you near Kapadiana, look for a turning off to the right (**1h55min**); there are waymark signs on the road and on a rock (you'll see them when you look back from just beyond them). Just off the road here is a leafy, cool, open area, where there is a spring. (*Walk 9, the ascent to Vrissinas, starts here.*) Have a rest in the shade if you like, then continue on into Kapadiana. The road forks: go right. The concrete road runs out and becomes a waymarked path; soon there are stone walls on either side. Pass a small church on your right (**2h10min**) and, just beyond it, the path leads onto track. Turn right and, five or six paces on, turn off left onto a lovely path leading through olive groves. All along the right-hand side of the path is a wooded ravine. The path opens out (**2h20min**) and you can see Chromonastiri straight ahead. Shortly afterward the path leads down onto a track. Turn left and follow the track round a bend; then, after about three minutes, take the first right turn, along an earthen track. Cross two small concrete bridges. Beyond an orange grove on your left, the track becomes a mostly-cobbled path again and starts climbing uphill towards the village.

When you meet a road (**2h45min**), cross over and walk past houses on a concreted track. In two to three minutes, rather than going straight on, take a left turn, which leads to the newer, unshaded square in Chromonastiri, where there are a couple of cafeneions. (There is a shady square closer to the village centre.) Head across the square, past a church on the left and an obelisk on the right, and turn left on the road beyond it (**2h55min**), to go downhill. Very soon, just after a shrine on the right, take the track off to the right. In spring masses of daisies line the route. When you meet the road again, continue downhill, following a wide bend to the right, round the end of a deep verdant ravine filled with chestnut and fig trees.

Ten minutes after joining the road you will see a stone church/shrine and steps leading off right (**3h20min**), down into the ravine. Take them and, at the bottom, as you come to the old church, go down right towards the water channel. There's a fresh water spring just beyond the church, should you want to fill your bottle. (Myli, the name of this ravine and the deserted village in it, comes from the many watermills in the area.) Follow the path that goes beside, in and over the water channel. When the path forks, go left over a concrete bridge and up the left-hand side of the ravine. To explore the ruined village of Myli, walk on for five minutes. Then return to this fork.

Once over the bridge, take the path heading up right, out of the ravine. When you are up on the road, turn right and walk uphill into the newer part of Myli, above the road to the left (**3h50min**), and order a taxi. Alternatively, walk (or hitch a lift) down to the coast, where you can pick up a city bus at Perivolia.

9 VRISSINAS, MINOAN PEAK SANCTUARY

See map pages 64-65   Distance: 6km/3.7mi; 2h45min

Grade: fairly strenuous climb and descent of 500m/1650ft

Equipment: stout shoes, sunhat, picnic, water, long trousers or socks

How to get there: 🚌 to Rethimnon (as Walk 8, page 66); then taxi to Kapadiana. Also: 🚌 from Rethimnon to Kapadiana (not in the timetables, but departs 06.50); journey time 30min. Or by 🚗: park on the track where the walk begins.

To return: 🚌 from Kapadiana, departs 14.30, then 🚌 from Rethimnon

This is one of those hikes that gives a great sense of achievement and a fantastic view. And it's particularly satisfying to see the mountain (858m/2815ft) from all around and know that you've been up there! The local people make pilgrimages to Vrissinas, which they know as Agios Pnevma, at Easter and other festivals. The summit was excavated in 1972 and samples of the large quantity of votive offerings that were found in rock clefts are now displayed at the Archaeological Museum in Rethimnon.

The walk begins about 200m/yds before the bus stop in Kapadiana — just where the road crosses a stream and changes from asphalt to concrete. Here a track (where you can park) heads south off the road. (If you've come by bus, walk back out of the village towards Roussospiti to this track, which will be on your left.) Follow the track to a drinking fountain housed in a small stone building 40 paces from the road, and a marble plaque with the date August 95 on a plane tree. These are useful landmarks, but unfortunately not visible from the road.

Beyond the spring the start of your cobbled path is obvious, leading uphill to the left; keep left within 30m/yds, where the rough cobbles end and a path appears to head off to the right. Within half a minute the path comes

Jerusalem sage lines the path to Vrissinas.

up onto a track, where you turn right uphill. Just after the first big bend to the left, take the track forking off to the right. You come to a large concrete cistern with red pipes (**10min**). Ignore two paths to the right of the cistern and take the cairned path which heads off to the left of it. It follows a ditch of sorts, next to a wire fence, for about six minutes. You pass through a wire gate; two minutes later, the wire fence you were walking beside blocks your way. Cross over to the left-hand side of the fence and continue on the cairned path. Six minutes later the path meets the cobbles of another path at a T-junction. Turn left on this path, which takes you along the edge of a ridge; a shallow gulley and old terracing is on your left.

Some **30min** into the walk you meet another track. The path crosses the track diagonally and continues on the far side. Head up the steep north side of the mountain, under shady oaks. In spring this part of the walk, shown on page 69, is thickly edged with glorious, bright yellow Jerusalem sage, and pretty mauve cistus is much in evidence.

Some **40 min** from the start the path divides. *Go left* (even if you spot faint blue waymarks enticing you to the right), and continue across and up the hillside on a well-defined path which traverses the north flank of Vrissinas, gently climbing. There are views of the Prassanos Gorge (Walk 7) and Mount Kouloukonas from here. About 20 minutes after the last junction, having *passed* the summit on your right, the route starts to zigzag up a gulley. Twelve minutes later the church at the top comes into view on your right. In another three minutes you meet a path at a T-junction: turn right on this path.

In five minutes you come to a stone building on your right (**1h15min**), with a water trough in front of it. From here there is no well-defined path up to the top — and it's a real scramble in places — but the church is in view so there is something to aim for! When faced with a choice in front of a rocky outcrop, the easiest way up is to go left around it. Twenty minutes from the stone building you are at the church* (**1h35min**), from where there are wonderful views over the north coast, Rethimnon, the White Mountains to the west and Mount Ida to the east.

Make your way back to the stone building, then return to Kapadiana on your outgoing path (**2h45min**). Pick up your transport, or perhaps walk on to Myli (see Walk 8).

*Just before the church *ignore* black and yellow (E4) arrow waymarking; it would take you to the south side of Vrissinas, and then too far east to locate your return path near the stone building.

10 GOUVERNETO AND KATHOLIKOU

See photograph page 26   **Distance:** 5km/3mi; 1h30min

Grade: moderate-strenuous, with a steep descent of 250m/800ft to Moni Katholikou and a reascent to Moni Gouverneto

Equipment: stout shoes, sunhat, picnic, water, swimming things, torch, suitable dress to enter the monastery (men should wear trousers and women longish skirts). *Note: Moni Gouverneto is closed from 14.00-17.00, but the quixotic powers-that-be sometimes close from 12.00!*

How to get there and return: 🚌 This walk is best approached by car (see Car tour 4, page 25). Otherwise it's a fairly long taxi journey. There are no conveniently-timed buses. Park at Moni Gouverneto.

The Akrotiri Peninsula, mushrooming out into the sea east of Hania, invites exploration. This walk follows an ancient path, originally traced by a hermit who, in the eleventh century, founded what is considered to be the island's earliest monastery, Moni Katholikou. It's a steep downhill route, but you can go on to the sea for a refreshing dip before climbing back up.

Leaving your car on the seaward side of Moni Gouverneto, **start out** by taking the path (by a hillock) leading down the hillside towards the sea. A red arrow on a shrine to your left will direct you initially. In **5min** you enjoy some lovely views (Picnic CT4). Continue down (sometimes on rough steps) and — by some ruins — leave the path and turn right to a cave (**10min**), with a chapel dedicated to Panagia Arkoudiotissa at its entrance and a huge, bear-shaped stalagmite in its centre.

Continuing the walk, go over a low rubble wall and head downhill left, towards a gap in the cliffs ahead. This path rejoins the one you left earlier, to see the cave. Turn right and continue down the hill. After **20min** the upper part of Moni Katholikou comes into sight. Reach another cave, halfway down a set of well-hewn steps. Near the bottom of the hill, a larger cave appears: this one contains, in its furthest recess, the grave of the hermit saint.

Now descend to the bridge below. Cross to the far left- or right-hand corner of the top of the bridge and scramble down the rocks to the dry streambed below; it leads to the sea. (Access is easier from the left corner, although on the way back it's easier getting up onto the bridge from the right.) By **45min** you will see the sea ahead. Getting to the water isn't very straight-forward just at the end of your descent, but walk round to the left, to an old slipway.

To return, retrace your steps back uphill (**1h30min**).

71

11 RODOPOS • AGIOS IOANNIS GIONIS • RODOPOS

See also photograph page 13   **Distance:** 18km/11.2mi; 5h45min
Grade: straightforward but taxing, with ups and downs totalling 500m/
1650ft. The initial descent is steep, and the final climb, while gradual,
is long. *There is hardly any shade en route.*
Equipment: stout shoes, sunhat, cover-up protection from the sun,
picnic, plenty of water
How to get there: 🚌 or 🚗 to Rodopos (not in the timetables, but departs
Hania 07.30, 13.30 in season; enquire locally); journey time 50min.
Or 🚗 to Kolimbari (Timetables 7, 8); journey time 30min, then 🚌 taxi
from there to Rodopos (the taxi rank is opposite the Hotel Rosmarie).
To return: 🚌 taxi from Rodopos to Kolimbari (telephone from the
cafeneion in the village square), then 🚗 to Hania (Timetables 7, 8).

One can't fail to notice the Rodopou Peninsula on the
map of Crete, jutting out into the sea with the Gramvousa Peninsula — rather like a rabbit's ears. The penin-
sulas invite exploration. This walk starts and finishes in
the very pleasant square in Rodopos village; all the locals
collect here to pass the time of day and watch the world
go by. You will be enveloped in quietness and a miles-
away-from-it-all feeling on this peninsula. The walk is
well waymarked, and few trees obscure the route. The
few trees, however, offer very little shade, so this is *not* a
hike to be undertaken in high summer. Getting into the
church of Agios Ioannis Gionis is not an essential part of
the walk but, if you wish to do so, ask for the key in Rodopos.

The bus turns round in the village square. **To start the
walk**, leave the square on your right and take the road
which leads out north past a bust, which is also on the
right, in a corner of the square. The road takes you past
a large church on the right. This church is a good landmark
when you return to the village from a
different direction, at the end of the walk.
Two to three minutes past the church,
nearing the edge of Rodopos, pass another
much smaller and very pretty church tucked
back on the right. Keep straight on.

Five minutes' walking will take you out
of the village. Ten minutes later (**15min**), the
road starts to bend, turning into motorable
track as it goes up and away from the village.
After the first big hairpin bend left look for
a path going uphill to the right, with a stone
wall on its left-hand side: it cuts some loops

*Some 25 minutes from Agios Ioannis Gionis, you look
down to the sea and another church, Agios Pavlos.*

off the track. When you meet the track again, head right. At **45min** the track passes through two concrete pillars (one may be collapsed). Ignore the lesser track heading off right beyond them; go straight ahead. Ten minutes later the sea is in sight behind you and to your right. Then these views are lost, as the track bends left and inland.

After **1h** walking a track peels off left; continue on the track you have been following and in another five minutes the sea will come into sight again over to the right. Soon two wells (an animal drinking place; **1h15min**) are ahead to the left and there is a sign in Greek indicating that the way to Agios Ioannis Gionis is to the right. The sign is for *vehicles*. Head off *left* beside the wells, on smaller track. One minute past the wells cross a track and continue straight over. Three minutes later come to a T-junction and go right. Continue round to the right and then, where the track forks a minute later, keep left uphill.

The track soon runs out (**1h25min**), in an open area where there is a building set down to the left. Walk straight ahead in the direction you have been heading. Then go right and find a waymark indicating a path leading to a low wall on which a metal shrine is bolted. Look over the wall and you will see the track you were originally following continuing downhill — to the dilapidated but attractively-sited church of Agios Ioannis Gionis far below. Secluded by trees and surrounded by open grazing land, the church is protected from the sea beyond by a ridge. To the left, the end of the Gramvousa Peninsula (photograph pages 18-19) is visible, reaching out into the sea. Take the footpath to the left of the low wall and wind

slowly downhill. Within a couple of turns you pass a miniature church perched on a rock.

Some 35 minutes of careful walking on the loose earth-and-rubble path will bring you to the flat area around Agios Ioannis Gionis (**2h15min**). To visit the church, cross the open ground in front of it. There are two concrete WCs to the left of it. The church is an obvious place to rest, in the welcome shade of a plane tree. Anyone and everyone who is called Ioannis can come here on one particular day the year to be baptised ... that's a lot of Johns!

From here go back to where the footpath ended and, with your back to the church, head to the right. In two minutes go through a fencing gate and, 10 minutes later, keep right when the track forks. Very soon Kastelli comes into view. Some 25 minutes from the church (**2h40min**) you look down to another church by the sea, Agios Pavlos, shown in the photograph on pages 72-73. At press date a track is being built down to this church, which will cut across your waymarked path. *Be prepared to spend some moments finding your ongoing route, waymarked with red paint daubs.* You need to keep parallel with the sea.

Some 1h20min from Agios Ioannis Gionis (**3h35min**) a few trees near a ravine provide rare and welcome shade. Below, the vivid blue sea curls tantalisingly up onto the rocky coastline. A patch of small carob trees, again by a ravine, offers a further brief shady interlude. Ten to 15 minutes beyond here the path curls uphill (**3h45min**). Look ahead, across the hillside, and you will see two footpaths crossing it: your path back to Rodopos is the higher one. A 30 minute climb lies ahead; keep looking for the sporadic waymarking as you cross the hillside.

Once back on level ground after this gruelling stretch, you come to grazing area. Imagine you are entering it at 6 o'clock. Ignore the gap and large boulder straight ahead;

walk towards 11 o'clock and look for cairns: they indicate your continuing route. Some 2h45min from Agios Ioannis Gionis (**5h**) you come to the end of the ridge on your left and meet a track. Go right, towards another grazing area. Having crossed this second, smaller stretch, head left on a track, rounding a vineyard. Five minutes later, at a T-junction, turn left. Very soon you see the sea and north coast. Five minutes later Rodopos is in sight straight ahead, with its easily-recognisable church. Stay on the track and, when concrete comes underfoot, go right. Then take the first left, up to the village square (**5h45min**).

12 RODOPOS • KOLIMBARI • MONI GONIA

See map pages 74-75   Distance: 6km/3.7mi;
Grade: a straightforward descent of about 250m/800ft, mostly on trac
Equipment: stout shoes, sunhat, picnic, water, suitable clothing for
visit to the monastery (trousers for men and longish skirts for women
Note: Moni Gonia is closed from 12.30-16.00 daily (Sat 07.00-16.00)
How to get there: 🚌 to Rodopos (as Walk 11, page 72).
To return: 🚌 from Kolimbari (Timetables 7, 8), or one of the freque
buses running from Kastelli to Hania.

This short but interesting foray into the Cretan countr
side combines the quiet attraction of hillside an
coastal villages, with an opportunity to visit a peacef
seaside monastery. Starting in Rodopos, where life go
on around the arena of an ample village square, the wa
goes through the smaller but very attractive village (
Astratigos, past and through fields, up and down a valle
to the sea at Kolimbari, a relaxed backwater just off th
main road within easy reach of Hania.

The bus turns round in Rodopos, which is also th
starting point for Walk 11. **Start out** by walking back o
the road (the way you came into the village). By the pen
ultimate house on the left, before the road bends to th
right, take the turn-off to the left (asphalted initially). Afte
you have turned onto it you will see a signpost on you
left for Astratigos (ΠΡΩΣ ΑΣΤΡΑΤΙΓΟ). Ignore the next turnin
left and keep straight on. Within a couple of minutes tak
the footpath climbing to the left; it cuts a bend off th
track. Rejoining the track at the top (by a shrine), go dow
to the right and you will see the coast spread out below

Soon, on a curve, where the domed church of Astra
tigos is ahead, bend right with the track. Then go left, ont
another track leading directly to the church. Leaving th
church on your left, head right, initially on a dirt track
Almost immediately take the path next to a stone wall.

*The harbour at
Kolimbari. Take a
break here at Mylos,
a pleasant café in a
converted mill by the
water's edge, opposit
the bakery/confect-
ionary. You can see
Moni Gonia from
here, in the
background.*

becomes a narrow concrete track as it leads down through the village of Astratigos. When it forks (at a junction, where there is the corner of a concrete building and a fence running off to the left of it in front of you), go left past some vegetable patches. Continue past a pine tree on the left, until you meet the road. Turn right. At the end of the village you approach the back of a road sign. Here turn left on a footpath which has a wall along its left side. Soon there are walls on both sides. Half a minute on, ignore a path off left; continue straight downhill towards the sea.

The path goes down one side of a small ravine and up the other side. You begin your descent into this ravine at about **30min**: follow a wall round to the left and keep it to your left. Three minutes later, just past a bend, you will see a small gate ahead: don't go through it. Leave it on the left; 6m/20yds below it, the path divides: turn right. The path curves down and to the right again, before crossing over the streambed. Head up to the left on the far side, walking just to the right of a boulder, and carry on uphill — on an overgrown and rather scratchy path. It's a four to five minute climb to the top.

Here, **45min** into the walk, the path joins a U bend of track and you will see the sea again. Go downhill to the right. Continue for 10 minutes; then, where the track joins another track, on a bend, go left. Stay on this main track until you come to a cross tracks, some 10 minutes later, where there is a large shrine on the left. Go straight across, now on concrete. The way heads downhill and, six minutes later, in amongst a rather unsightly band of houses, the track becomes road just before a junction. This is Grimbiliana, the heart of which is an attractive old village.

Take the first turning left; the road curves round to the right and comes to a junction with an asphalt road. Turn left and head down towards the sea. At **1h25min** the road forks between the houses of Kolimbari, almost at sea level: keep right. This brings you into the middle of the village. Head left towards Moni Gonia, a 10-minute walk away. But first, when you come to a building on the right with columns, turn down towards the harbour shown opposite.

After visiting Moni Gonia, walk back through the village, keep left at the post office, and continue to the main crossroads, where you can catch a bus from opposite the Hotel Rosmarie (**2h**). (The Rosmarie's proprietor played an active role during the Second World War. His brave efforts are catalogued by newspaper cuttings on display in the hotel. Rosmarie was the gentleman's code name.)

13 FROM SIRIKARI TO POLIRINIA

See map pages 82-83   **Distance:** 8km/5mi; 2h40min

Grade: moderate, with a steep initial descent of about 300m/1000ft, then an easy gorge walk and a gentle ascent of about 200m/650ft

Equipment: stout shoes, sunhat, picnic, water

How to get there: 🚌 to Kastelli (Timetable 8); journey time 45min. Change to Sirikari 🚌 (not in the timetables, but departs Mondays to Fridays at 12.30 (call Kastelli bus station to check: 0822-22035); journey time 1h

To return: 🚌 from Polirinia to Kastelli (Mon, Wed, Fri only; journey time 15min) or 🚕 taxi — organise this before you leave Kastelli (0822-22225) or ask at a taxi rank. Then 🚌 from Kastelli (Timetable 8)

The gorge leading to Polirinia is wide, pretty and peaceful in the extreme — filled with bright yellow Jerusalem sage in spring and crisp pink and white oleander in summer. And a bonus to this delightful walk is a visit to Kastelli, a very pleasant town where the local people are particularly charming and helpful. Taking a morning bus from Hania gives you time to wander round Kastelli, before catching your onward bus to Sirikari — a journey affording splendid views, as you wind into the heart of the countryside.

Get off the bus where it turns round at the end of its journey, by a solitary church. **Start out** by walking straight across from the church gate. A stock control gate indicates the route, and it is waymarked, as is the path leading to it. After **5min** take the footpath branching left; it heads more steeply downhill and might be a bit overgrown in spring. Follow waymarking through an olive grove (it may be necessary to scramble down in places). Ten minutes later you emerge on a track from where you can see a multi-levelled house below you, on the far side of the valley. It's a good landmark as the path runs onwards just in front of it.

Cross straight over the track, picking up the waymarked path on the other side. Very soon the path forks; take the right-hand fork and a few minutes later go through a stock control gate (there are electricity wires close overhead), then turn left immediately. A few minutes later, go through another stock control gate and down a dozen or so stone steps, to a track. Cross the track and the riverbed just beyond it — the latter will become the gorge that this walk follows. Walk up towards the house you saw earlier and turn right on the dirt track just in front of it. Fifty metres/yards along, take a path leading off left (past the collapsed stone wall of a terrace). The path is perfectly obvious from here on and there is plenty of waymarking

These pleasant hills are the setting for Picnic 13.

en route. Be sure to leave any stock control gates as you find them. The path leads back down to the riverbed, which is lined with leafy plane trees, and before long passes a small ramshackle bridge off to the right. By now the route is within the beginnings of the gorge, and the air is light and fresh. The route cuts an arm off the riverbed, then continues along the left-hand side of it. Head on towards some water troughs (**1h**) and, just beyond them, cross the riverbed diagonally and go up onto the far bank.

In **1h30min** the path has taken you well up the right-hand side of the gorge, and the landscape has opened up. Soon, another valley meets this one from the right, and the village of Polirinia can be seen ahead in the distance, its church set on the heights. Cross a pretty, old cobbled bridge (**1h35min**) and continue parallel with the riverbed, now on your right, past some fencing. The path soon widens into a track, passing a concrete pumphouse (**1h50min**) on the left.

Follow the main track, ignoring any sharp turnings to the left or right. At the Y-shaped junction near the **2h05min**-mark, take the right fork — there *is* waymarking, but you have to look out for it. Soon pass the first houses of Polirinia. This is a pleasant setting for a countryside picnic (Picnic 13; see photograph above). Five minutes beyond the houses you will be rounding a right-hand bend, where there is a rock on the right consisting of hundreds of slate-like layers: look here for a steep narrow path (also on the right) that curves up to the right. Take it; it soon becomes cobbled. A few minutes later you emerge in a paved square with a water trough and truncated tree in its centre. From here head up left between the houses. Carry straight on, ignoring the steps to the right, and following the telephone poles instead. At the top, turn left and stay on the track. Come to the village cafeneion (**2h40min**), where the bus turns round (and a taxi or friends could meet you).

14 KATSOMATADOS • MOURI • VOULGARO

Distance: 13km/8mi; 3h20min

Grade: easy-moderate, with an initial ascent of about 250m/800ft, followed by a descent (sometimes a scramble) of 450m/1500ft

Equipment: stout shoes, sunhat, picnic, water

How to get there: Elafonisi 🚌 to Katsomatados (not in the timetables, but departs 08.00 *in summer only;* check at the KTEL office in Hania); journey time 1h10min. Or 🚌 to Kastelli (Timetable 8); journey time 45min, then 🚌 to Katsomatados (not in the timetables, departs 14.00); journey time 20min. Or by 🚗: park in Katsomatados square.
To return: 🚌 from Voulgaro to Kastelli (not in the timetables, departs 17.10 daily); journey time 10min, then 🚌 to Hania (Timetable 8). Do *not* rely on the return Elafonisi bus, since it may well be full and not stop. Alternatively, if you travelled by car to Katsomatados, take a 🚗 taxi from Voulgaro back to Katsomatados, to pick up your car (enquire at the first cafeneion you come to in Voulgaro, called 'H ΑΝΑΤΟΛΗ', on the right-hand side of the road).

A fine wedge of western Crete's countryside — some lovely and varied landscapes — are covered in this walk. We take you through a gorge, along a pretty chestnut tree-lined valley, into some sweeping open countryside, and finally down a ravine well used by grazing flocks of sheep and goats. There's some scrambling en route, but for the most part the walk is on well-defined track.

If you take a taxi from Kastelli, the driver will stop for you to look down into the Topolia Gorge before dropping you on the outskirts of Katsomatados; otherwise you can see the gorge walls quite well from the bus. If travelling by bus, ask to be dropped off about 350m/yds beyond the approach sign for the village of Katsomatados. (The village sign clearly says 'Koutsoumatados', but the villagers are adamant that this is a newfangled and ugly name, so we have obliged them.) Here, not far past a cafeneion with a shady terrace opposite it, a concrete track leads down into the village (signposted: 'square, taverna, parking').

Start the walk by leaving the main road on this track, going over a bridge and past the large taverna called 'Hiker' (with rooms to rent), on the left. Go straight ahead, over a water channel, and onto a rough track. Pass a pretty church on the left and continue along the very pleasant, shady track. Plane trees and chestnuts, olives and olean-der keep everything cool, growing as they do along the watercourse on the left. Anywhere along here is pleasant for picnicking (Picnic 14). We are in the valley shown in the centre of the photograph opposite, a lush green setting. Ignore first a right and then a left fork (the latter crossing over the streambed); keep the streambed on your left. At **15min** you come to a stock control gate: leave it as you nd it. The track starts to climb and, five minutes later, is oncreted for about 40m/yds, as it bends sharp left uphill.

You will walk out of the shade as the track becomes much wider, leading through open countryside, with gentle green hills all round. Pass a stone shelter to the left and then half a dozen wooden feeding troughs. Go through a break in a mesh fence just beyond the troughs. 's a 30-minute climb to the top, from where there are wonderful views, as you can see in the photograph below.

wenty minutes from the troughs you come to an inter-ection where the choice is a gradual right bend going ownhill or a sharp right bend going uphill: follow the atter. Five minutes later, at the saddle, ignore the two racks going off left and right; go straight ahead through stock control gate (**50min**). Keep on the track as it bends ound to the left, ignoring two tracks going off sharply to ne right (the first one leads down to Sasalos; Walk 15). A few minutes along the route you can see the village of asalos, below on the right.

Eight minutes past the view over Sasalos, your track orks downhill to the left (ignore a newer and wider track which carries on straight ahead). You pass a fenced vine-yard on the left and some olive trees on the right. In five minutes you will be facing a mesh fence blocking the path

We've climbed high enough now to look back to the village of Katso-matados, seen below in the valley. Walk 15 enjoys this same view on the descent to Katsomatados and Topolia. Picnic 14 is set be-low in the valley.

to the streambed directly in front of you. If you hav
difficulty climbing over it, look for easier access over t
the right and make your way to the church of Agio
Athanasios on the far bank. From here a well-defined pat
runs diagonally back to the streambed.

Once in the streambed (**1h15min**), head north
northeast along it; a rough path leads you beside, in an
over the dry watercourse. Goats and sheep wander abou
and sit in the shade, close to the piped water runnin
along the route. The streambed becomes a ravine a b
further on, where the animals shelter from the sun. Walk
ing here in spring and early summer you'll find a mass c
pungent dragon lilies standing sentry, together with thic
Jerusalem sage. At **1h30min** come to a point where yo
can see through high, sloping rock walls to the countrysid

beyond. The route then
starts to descend steeply, as
the streambed becomes a
ravine. It's necessary to
scramble in places. Keep to
the left-hand side and, five
minutes later, at the narrowest point, a stock control fence bars the way:
negotiate it and continue
downhill, picking your
own route. Within 10 min-
utes you emerge on a track
that crosses the water-
course: turn left.

In early summer you
will be surrounded by
bright yellow broom; in
autumn the yellows and
golds of vineyards lend
mellow overtones to the
landscape. Soon, beyond
another stock control gate,
keep on the main track,
ignoring any turning to the
left or right. After about 30
minutes, the track — more
of a dirt road by now —
becomes asphalted, and
you meet a fork: walk
downhill to the right.

Within a few minutes you will pass the first houses of Mouri, a very small village. Before long, pass an old cafeneion on the right (**2h25min**), shaded by vines and mulberries. Keep ahead on the asphalt road, passing a church on your left as you leave Mouri.

Twenty minutes from the cafeneion, the road winds down into the tiny hamlet of Katohori, looping round a concrete, red-tiled church en route. Voulgaro can be seen across the valley and, a bit further on, the village of Topolia comes into view, with the narrow gorge leading to Katsomatados to its left. The road eventually bends right round a small white-washed barrel-vaulted church. Twenty minutes later, you emerge on the main road through Voulgaro. Turn right into the village (**3h20min**) and head for the nearest cafeneion, to enquire about buses or taxis.

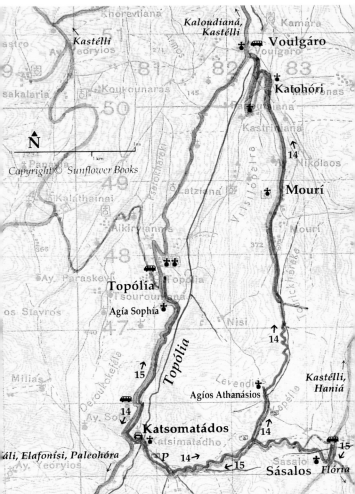

15 SASALOS • KATSOMATADOS • TOPOLIA

See map pages 82-83; see also photograph page 81

Distance: 8km/5mi; 2h15min

Grade: easy, with an ascent of 200m/650ft and descent of 250m/800ft

Equipment: stout shoes, sunhat, picnic, water

How to get there: 🚌 to Kasteili (Timetable 8); journey time 45min; then 🚌 to Sasalos (not in the timetables, departs 14.00 daily); journey time approximately 1h. Or 🚕 taxi from Kastelli to Sasalos.
To return: 🚌 from Topolia to Kastelli (not in the timetables, departs 15.30 daily); journey time 30min; or 🚕 taxi to Kastelli. Then 🚌 to Hania (Timetable 8); journey time 45min

Short walk: Sasalos — Katsomatados (5km/3mi; 1h35min). Grade, equipment, access as main walk. Follow the main walk to Katsomatados and there either hail a 🚕 taxi on the main road outside the village or call for one from one of the cafeneions on the main road.

Taking a straightforward route from Sasalos to Topolia, this walk makes a delightful afternoon's ramble. The countryside stays green throughout the summer, oleanders cover the hillsides, and leafy chestnut trees line and shade the country track for part of the way. Give yourselves plenty of time to wander around Kastelli before taking the onward bus to Sasalos.

No matter where the bus stops, **start out** by walking on into Sasalos, passing a sign indicating 'Floria' (ΦΛΩΡΙΑ) to the left. Then go right, over a bridge and, just past a building on the right, turn right on an earthen track. Walk past an old barn-like building set back from the road and head towards the church shown below. At the church, turn right along the watercourse and follow the track through the trees. When you meet another track coming

from the village, join it and head left uphill. Ignore any turn-offs.

Eventually, the track levels out (**40min**). You can see the track to Voulgaro (Walk 14) ahead, making a long bend to the right. Look for a short, steep stretch of track heading left and sharply back. Follow it. Go through the stock

Before setting out, have a look at this pretty church in Sasalos. Its dome is no longer painted blue.

The harbour at Hania

control gate at the top and you will find yourself looking down from the ridge — with views over the fertile hills spreading out ahead into the distance (photograph page 81). Three tracks lead off from here: take the middle one; it bends down to a valley which leads to Katsomatados.

A few minutes later you meet another fork. Head left on the track that goes down towards the bottom of the valley. Some 25 minutes from the top of the ridge, beyond half a dozen feeding troughs and a stone animal shelter on the right, the track enters the tree line. Ignore a footpath signposted to 'Kastanodasos' (an old chestnut wood) and follow the track as it turns down to the right and crosses the stream. Continue straight downhill, shaded by leafy chestnuts. Just before entering Katsomatados, you will pass a very pretty church on the right and then a large taverna called 'Hiker' (**1h30min**).

Continue straight ahead. Cross the bridge over the riverbed and bend left with the concrete track, up onto the main asphalt road. Turn right here and walk to Topolia, 40 minutes away. Some 350m/yds from the junction there are a couple of cafeneions, just past a bend. The Short walk ends here; either wait for a taxi to pass or telephone for one. The main walk keeps along the road; soon you will see a tunnel cutting into the Topolia Gorge wall. A few minutes before the tunnel entrance, an old sign in Greek indicates Agia Sophia (Αγ Σοφια). This is a church built inside a cave; it's just a short climb off the road (a star at the mouth of the cave is just visible from the road). Having made the effort to climb up ... or not, continue along the main road, negotiating the tunnel carefully. It's not very long; in fact you can see light at the far end of it. The Gorge of Topolia runs deep to the right of the road. About 200m/yds from the tunnel exit you can admire the view from a small cantina overlooking the gorge. When you arrive at Topolia (**2h15min**) hail a passing taxi. There are usually taxis parked somewhere on the main road in this top part of the village. Or, if you started the walk early (perhaps had a lift), you may be in time for the 15.30 bus.

16 THE AGIA IRINI GORGE

Distance: 9.5km/6mi; 3h30min

Grade: straightforward gorge walk descending about 600m/2000ft; waymarked. There are some short steep sections where surefootedness and a modicum of agility are required. Possibility of vertigo in two places if safety railings are not in place. Plenty of shade.

Equipment: stout shoes, sunhat, picnic, water, swimming things

How to get there: Sougia 🚐 (Timetable 6); ask to get off at the Irini Gorge ('faráji') itself, or at Agia Irini (then walk south downhill for 10min to the gorge) or at Epanohori (then walk 7min north uphill to the gorge); journey time 1h15min

To return: 🚐 from Sougia (Timetable 6); journey time 1h30min

The Irini Gorge has been made easily passable by mechanics and man, perhaps to take some pressure off the Samaria Gorge — and perhaps to make another tourist haunt! Although there are seating areas and drinking water is available, the gorge is still very much in its natural state. At press date some of the railings were not yet in place, but they should be when you use this book. Although not as dramatic as Samaria, Irini makes a good walk most of the year, and Sougia is a pleasant, somewhat sleepy, backwater at which to end up and have a swim before the return journey. Alternatively you could stay overnight there, walk via Lisos to Paleohora the next day (Walk 17) or even carry on from Paleohora to Elafonisi (Walk 18) and get a bus back to Hania from there.

Start the walk by the large signboard on the left on the road to Sougia; you are on rough track. Just after some small buildings (ticket offices/rest rooms) the streambed starts on your left-hand side. Pines scent the air, and chestnut trees provide leafy cover. Seven minutes into the walk the track crosses the streambed and before long becomes a path, as it rises above the streambed again. From now on it is straightforward, waymarked walking, with several 'official' places to rest and plenty of unofficial pleasant spots to sit and admire a major rockfall or simply enjoy the scenery.

By **2h30min** you will be aware that the gorge is ending, as you look ahead to hillsides. When there are olive groves on either side of you (**2h40min**), the waymarked route heads uphill to the left, out of the riverbed and onto a dirt track. Head right and 10 minutes later come to a cross-track. Up to the left is a church, and down to the right an old bridge, in the middle of the riverbed. Keep straight ahead, following the riverbed on your right. At just over **3h** meet an asphalted road and turn right over a bridge. Soon the road climbs up to the main Sougia road: turn left and walk the last 2.5km to the sea (**3h30min**).

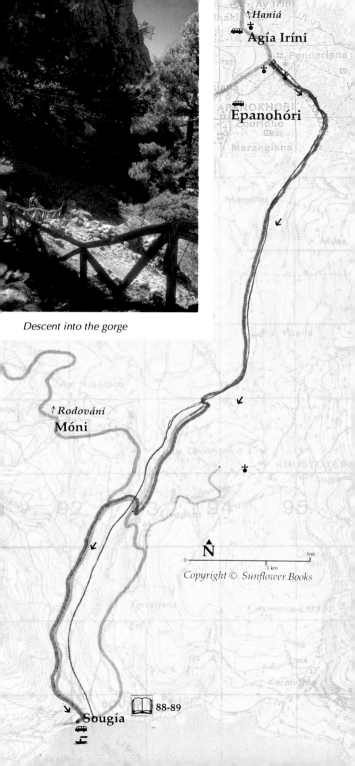

Descent into the gorge

↑*Haniá*

Agía Iríni

Pendariana

APINOKHORI

Epanohóri

Marangiana

↑*Rodováni*

Móni

N

0   1 km   1mi

Copyright © Sunflower Books

88-89

Sougía

17 SOUGIA • LISOS • PALEQHORA

Map continues on pages 90-91; see also photograph page 21
Distance: 17km/10.5mi; 4h45min
Grade: moderate-strenuous, with ups and downs totalling about 400m/1300ft; E4 waymarked throughout
Equipment: stout shoes, sunhat, long socks/trousers, picnic, ample water
How to get there: 🚌 to Sougia (Timetable 6); journey time 1h30min
To return: 🚌 from Paleohora (Timetable 5); journey time 2h
Short walk: Sougia — Lisos — Sougia (8km/5mi; 2h30min). Moderate climb and descent of 150m/500ft; equipment and access as main walk. Return on 🚌 from Sougia (Timetable 6); journey time 1h30min

The bus ride to Sougia, where this walk starts, is through a picturesque wooded valley and tree-clad hillsides — the western foothills of the White Mountains — glorious in autumn colours. The bus follows the Agia Irini Gorge (Walk 16) and riverbed down to the Libyan Sea. This sea is ever in view throughout the walk, which parallels the coast. The first stage takes you through an exceedingly pretty gorge, then uphill, over, and down to the ancient Roman site at Lisos, set back from the sheltered bay of Agios Kyrkos. The second pull brings us up and across a large, flat-topped headland, before we head back down to the sea and along a length of coast, punctuated by bays, stretching all the way to Paleohora.

The bus will drop you beside the sea in Sougia. A sweep of shingle beach stretches out in front of you. Facing the sea, **start off** by heading right (west) from the bus and car park. Keep round to the right when the route divides at Sougia's small harbour. A rock face rears up in front of you, and a sign points you in the direction of Lisos. The path is E4 waymarked and leads into the very pretty gorge shown on page 21, thick with brilliant pink oleander in late spring and summer. There are ideal picnic places all along this gorge (Picnic 17). Choose your spot — under carobs, olives or pines, in the gorge or beside it.

Just **25min** into the walk, the smooth gorge walls tower up above you. Five minutes later, look up left: the path

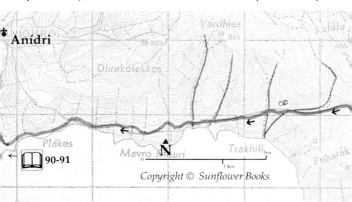

Copyright © Sunflower Books

High above Lisos we cross a plateau covered with spiny broom and spurge, before descending to Paleohora on the coast.

which you must follow leaves the gorge. Some **50min** into the walk you will see Lisos below you, set back from its lovely sheltered bay. The waymarked path twists downhill; you pass the mouth of a cave (**1h**) set up on the right of the path. The main site of Lisos is reached in about **1h15min**. If the site isn't open, look for the keeper, who can usually be found in his nearby house that doubles up as a refreshment hut. The Short walk ends here at Lisos; return by the same route to Sougia.

To continue to Paleohora, follow the waymarking and in under **2h** you should be well within sight of the south coast and your destination. There are some lovely coves in which to swim and enjoy the solitude. By **3h35min** you come upon a long sweep of beach, no doubt dotted with visitors people getting an all-over tan. Just over an hour later you will be in Paleohora (**4h45min**). The bus turns round and stops just before the main street narrows, beyond a statue to Konstantin Kriaris. (There is a clock tower beyond this narrow part of the street.)

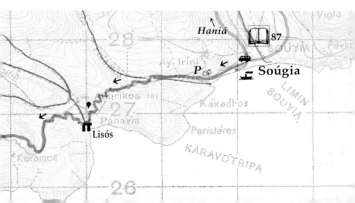

18 FROM PALEOHORA (KRIOS BEACH) TO ELAFONISI

See photograph page 4   **Distance:** 9.5km/5.9mi; 3h30min

Grade: moderate, with ups and downs totalling about 200m/650ft, but you must be sure-footed and agile, with a head for heights (possibility of vertigo). E4 waymarked throughout

Equipment stout shoes, sunhat, picnic, ample water

How to get there: 🚌 to Paleohora (Timetable 5); journey time 2h (or walk from Sougia; Walk 17); then 🚕 taxi to Krios Beach (7km)
To return: 🚌 from Elafonisi at 16.00 or 🚌 from Moni Chrisoskalitisas at 18.00 (not in the timetables; *in high summer only*). Or 🚢 back to Paleohora; departs 16.00, 18.00 *in high summer only*.

This is a lovely coastal walk, with the sound of the sea accompanying you all the way. Paleohora is a pleasant place to stay — or spend the night if you've walked from Sougia (Walk 17). It has a good bookshop, and several tavernas and café-bars where you would undoubtedly meet other walkers. Once you reach Elafonisi, you could walk 5km along the rough road to Moni Chrisoskalitisas,

visit it, then catch the 18.00 bus back to Hania from there.

The taxi will drop you by a cantina at the edge of Krios Beach. Leaving the cantina on your right, **start the walk** by heading west across the beach towards the headland; you might find yourself getting your feet wet as you round a rock by the first E4 waymark post. It is at the foot of a rocky path which heads up the hillside and is marked with yellow and then red waymarks. Some **10min** along you will be at the top of the first headland, looking back at the beach and the sad sight of acres of plastic green-houses beyond it — all too common along the south coast of Crete — and an unsightly contrast to the lovely sea.

In another ten minutes cross over the top of the next headland; a peninsula juts out into the sea in the distance. At **1h** the path crosses quite loose scree, and there is no protection from the drops down to the sea — a vertiginous patch of path. Ten minutes later, having crossed another ridge, the chapel of Agios Ioannis comes into sight. Outside it, there is a huge, inviting bell to ring — and the door is not locked. If you find it hard to spot the next E4 sign, look for a cairn or old red waymark. Another vertiginous section is encountered at **1h40min**. Five minutes later the route seems to head uphill away from the edge of the cliff, but walk to the edge: you may be alarmed to see an E4 sign *below* you. There is a way down! It requires some ten minutes' careful scrambling down onto a beach. Cairns and red waymarks mark the way across the beach.

The route on to Elafonisi continues to be waymarked sporadically but your direction is clear. Some **3h30min** from the start, if you've timed your walk to coincide with the boat back to Paleohora, you will see it moored, on its own, off the rocks to your left; a small sign indicates departure times. Beyond are the beaches, cantinas, and car park of Elafonisi. The bus back to Hania leaves from behind the last cantina you come to.

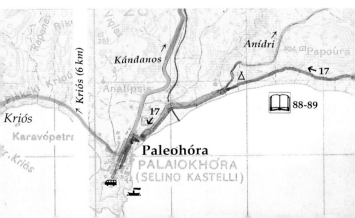

19 XILOSKALA • LINOSELI COL • GINGILOS • XILOSKALA

See map pages 96-97   Distance: 13km/8mi; 5-6h

Grade: strenuous climb and descent of 850m/2800ft; you must be sure-footed and agile, and have a head for heights (danger of vertigo)

Equipment: walking boots, anorak, sunhat, picnic, ample water

How to get there and return: 🚌 or 🚐 to/from Omalos (Timetable 3); journey time about 45min (Xiloskala is the last stop, at the top of the Samaria Gorge). We have been assured that the company puts a bus on if there are people travelling, *regardless of the season.*

Shorter walk: Xiloskala — Linoseli Col — Xiloskala (10km/6.2mi; 3h30min); grade, equipment, access/return as main walk. Follow the main walk for 1h40min and return the same way. Slightly less strenuous climb and descent of 500m/1650ft.

By climbing Gingilos you can totally immerse yourself in the deep solitude, silence, echoes and majesty characteristic of high mountain walks. Gingilos is a magnificent and awesome mass, towering to one side of the Samaria Gorge. Wild rock formations, a massive band of scree, echoing stone walls, wild flowers clinging peri-lously to ledges, contorted, windswept trees, and breath-taking views are just some of this walk's delights.

Walking to the Linoseli Col (the Shorter walk) will probably be more than enough of an experience for some of you. Intrepid types can clamber to the top of Gingilos. The walk is easier than it looks when you stand and con-template the mountain; Gingilos (2080m/6820ft) may not be the highest peak on Crete, but it's certainly one of the most inspiring.

The bus turns round at Xiloskala, the top of the walk down into the Samaria Gorge (Walk 21; Walk 20 also begins here). Facing the wooden railings at the top of the 'xiloskala' (Greek for wooden staircase like the one shown in the photograph on page 87), look right, up towards a small rest house perched on the hillside, off the road. The hike to Gingilos starts behind that building. **Set off** up the path leading towards the rest house and round to the right of it. Look for the brown and yellow sign, to the right of the top storey of the building. It points to the 'Linoseli Footpath'. The path climbs steeply, so you gain height rapidly. There are occasional trees at the side of the path, giving shade for pauses, and a fence edges it along one side.

At **30min** into the walk, the path goes through a large gap in the fence, beyond which it flattens out. You are now heading well away from the Omalos, which is fast receding behind you. Where the path begins to run high

— and there is a fair drop to the left side (**45min**) vertigo sufferers may feel anxious. Looking back from here gives you an excellent view of the refuge high up at Kallergi, on the far side of the Samaria Gorge (see photograph on page 95). Notice from here two paths in particular: one in the foreground comes down to Xiloskala (Walk 20); the other, in the middle distance (to the right of Kallergi) leads through the conservation area into the Samaria Gorge.

Our path now takes us under a huge rock arch (**50min**); Cretan ebony hangs gracefully from it, and you cannot fail to feel as though you're in the very heart of the mountains here. There are massive, dramatic rock faces, peaks, boulders and formations all around, as the photograph below shows.

Dramatic rock formations characterise the exhilarating hike to Gingilos.

At **1h** into the walk you round a very large rock on the right; you will notice a shallow cave beneath it. Five minutes later, the route leads to the Linoseli Spring, where a water tank is tucked into the rock. The path goes on and up to the right, towards the massive scree slope shown on page 93, and a very obvious peak beyond it, pointing up into the sky. After the first bend, pick up a waymarked route which zigzags on up the mountain. Parts of it are on a firm scree base and there are cairns en route as well. Some 18 minutes past the Linoseli Spring, the path flattens out for a short distance. A large rock offers some shade.

Eventually (**1h40min**) you will reach a distinct ridge, the Linoseli Col. Here it may well be very windy indeed, but the thrill of being up so high and seeing for miles and miles is terrific. On a clear day, looking back to Kallergi, you might just be able to pick out Theodorou Island to the left of the refuge, off the distant north coast.

The Shorter walk returns from this col to Xiloskala via the same route, but for those who wish to tackle the summit, the climb starts from this ridge. Look left to find an arrow pointing up the edge of the mountain. Follow the waymarking — do not lose sight of it — and it will lead you steeply upwards. In places it is necessary to clamber and scramble; you need to be very surefooted and confident. *Caution:* After about 2-300m/yds there is a pit almost 25m/80ft deep just beneath the marked path — it's about 2.5m/8ft in diameter, and the sides are sheer. *Beware!* Before long you will have a simply splendid view over the Omalos again and, by **2h25min**, the route will become easier as you near the top. Five minutes later, you will reach a cairn on a flattened area that feels like the top. In fact, the very highest point (Volakias) is 30 minutes away. Press on if you feel the urge — we did not, because the way is not marked.

When you have taken in the tremendous view, make your way back to the ridge by carefully following the way-marking from the first cairn on the flat. It offers a choice of routes, some easier than others. Use your discretion, knowing where you are heading. Fifty minutes later you will be back at the Linoseli Col. It's pleasant, on the way down, to be able to pay more attention to the spectacular landscape and the trees — among them the pretty Montpelier maple. The descent back to Xiloskala takes about 2h30min (**5-6h**). If you sit on the rest house terrace having a drink, make sure you are ready to jump on the bus: it arrives, turns round and leaves almost immediately.

20 A HIGH MOUNTAIN CIRCUIT FROM KALLERGI

Distance: 16km/10mi; 5h35min

Grade: for experienced mountain walkers; strenuous, with overall ascents/descents of about 600m/2000ft. Some of the route is part of the E4 trail, but our walk describes a circuit returning to Kallergi.

Equipment: walking books, anorak, sunhat, headscarf, compass, picnic, ample water

How to get there and return: 🚐 4WD vehicle to/from Kallergi, or stay overnight there (see 'Where to stay', page 40). Alternatively, 🚌 or 🚐 to/from Xiloskala (see Walk 19, page 92). From Xiloskala, you will have to walk to and from Kallergi (add 2h; see Short walk below)

Short walk: Xiloskala — Kallergi — Xiloskala (8km/5mi; 2h). Easy track walking for most of the way. Stout shoes, sunhat, picnic, water. Access/return: as Walk 19, page 92. See notes page 98.

A breathtaking hike in more ways than one, the trek to Melindaou is, without doubt, worth the effort. The lure of the high mountains is a compelling experience, and this walk — in the heart of the splendid Levka Ori (White Mountains) — is an exciting introduction to high mountain walking on Crete.

This expedition requires stamina. You must also be sure-footed and know how to use a compass competently. The rewards are ample, and walking in this area, we are sure, will mean the beginning of a long association with Crete's mountains. You will carry the views with you forever — the space, the fold upon fold of rock and mountainside, the colours and textures, the height, depth and strength of western Crete.

Before setting off, be sure to tell someone at Kallergi where you are going. Then **start out**: walk the length of

The Kallergi refuge sits perched atop a peak, in line with Gingilos; between these peaks, the Samaria Gorge slices its way to the sea.

the refuge and follow the short path leading to a track. This track heads off east towards the mountains. You will follow it to the Poria ('Shepherds' Saddle'). The route affords a tremendous view of Kallergi and Gingilos; see photograph on page 95. Some **20min** from Kallergi, when the hut is completely out of sight, and the valley falls away to the left of the track, you will have a wonderful view of mountains ... and still more mountains. From here,

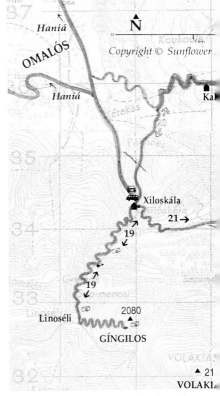

Copyright © Sunflower

on a clear day, it is possible to see all the way to Theodorou Island off the north coast, west of Hania.

By **45min** from Kallergi, rounding a bend in the track, you will be at a saddle, called 'Poria' by the shepherds. From here paths lead in different directions. Before going down towards the open area to the right of the track, look further ahead to see the shepherds' dwellings on the left. At the end of this walk, you will come down off the mountainside opposite these dwellings. Then continue: turn right off the track and head across the centre of the open area on a path, making for a stone igloo-shaped structure (with jagged rocks in the distance beyond it). Gingilos is just visible behind the jagged fringe. Pass the stone shelter and then look for the first left turn. It bends back away from the view to Kallergi and takes you across the hillside. A slight knoll is seen on the highest point ahead of you. You are heading east. Seven minutes later, continue in an easterly direction, leaving a huge square boulder off to the left. Follow waymarking as you climb more and more steeply. To check your whereabouts, look back to Kallergi some 20 minutes into the climb. You will

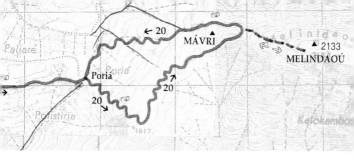

see a blasted tree trunk. It is a striking sight against the hillside.

After **1h30min** — the last half of which involves a very steep climb — the route flattens out briefly; you will be level with the refuge, now far in the distance. This respite doesn't last long, however, and the route continues on and up, beyond a substantial cairn. Fifteen minutes later, reach the top of the first ridge, from where you can feast your eyes upon yet more splendid mountains and the inspiring Cretan landscape.

Head left along the ridge in a northeasterly direction and follow the waymarking carefully. Within a short distance find the first of several cairns. Continue along the ridge. By **2h10min** you'll start climbing again. *Follow the waymarking assiduously.* Ten minutes later come to a short concrete pillar, with three bits of iron protruding from it. From this point you can see the route leading across another ridge towards Mavri (the photograph on page 98 was taken here and shows the route clearly). Thirteen minutes later (**2h25min**), locate another cairn on the ridge. Go straight up the ridge and, at **2h30min** (at the next cairn, near the top of Mavri), take the path curving round to the right across to the next slope.

At **2h40min**, having gone halfway along the ridge, look for a path heading sharply back to the left, round the other side of Mavri. This is the homeward route. You can either head back now or press on further and follow the path as it continues towards Melindaou's summit (see photograph caption on page 98).

There is no obvious point of return if you continue to Melindaou; the path leads on even further into the White Mountains, to Pahnes, the highest peak in the range — a couple of days' and nights' trek away. So unless you're with a guide, it's best to opt for the homeward path, identified after passing Mavri. It cuts a route lower down and back across the mountainside, in the direction of Kallergi. Follow the waymarking over a ridge and look down to the right, along the valley ahead: you will spot a clear

The walker is a mere dot in the landscape on this high mountain walk which circles Mavri (the central peak). Melindaou is to the right.

path running along the valley. Pick your way carefully down towards the path and the valley floor — a rough descent lasting 15 minutes.

Once on the floor of the valley, waymark arrows will guide you back to the track just beyond the Poria, where you started up the mountainside. In April and May the valley floor is swathed in crocuses and wildflowers — a heartening sight for the trek back to Kallergi. Well into the return journey, the path crosses a dried-up water course and continues unevenly all the way back to the track where the shepherds' dwellings stand as a landmark 150m/yds from the Poria. From here, retrace your steps to Kallergi (**5h35min**); the sense of achievement is terrific.

Short walk (to Kallergi)

Kallergi is the mountain refuge in the Levka Ori that hikers and climbers use as a base for exploring the range, under the guidance and supervision of the refuge's professional Austrian management. However, you don't have to be an expert to enjoy its spectacular position, perched like an eyrie at 1677m/5470ft above sea level. The refuge provides an authentic retreat from the noisy world we live in and offers either basic or more pampered living accommodation and facilities. You can spend a night — by prior arrangement — or simply visit to marvel at the views, enjoy a picnic and revel in the peaceful atmosphere of the mountains.

To get there, first walk to the wooden railings by the viewpoint overlooking the Samaria Gorge, and look to the left of the gorge entrance. You will see a stone bench, set against a wall beneath a large conifer. Start off on the path leading away from behind this tree. It crosses the hillside, climbing very gradually at first and running almost parallel with the car park below. At a three-way fork (8min) take the branch furthest to the left. You climb quite steeply round the head of a shallow ravine down to the left (15min). Look back across the car park and beyond the tourist pavilion, to Gingilos, the impressive grey mass in the background. As the path which you are on rounds the shoulder of the hill, the Omalos comes into view, spread out like a tablecloth far below.

Continue on the path until it meets track on a hairpin bend (25min). A small cairn marks the junction; this waymarker is a help on the return journey. Head to the right up the rough track. Half an hour later you will reach the top. There is a shrine and an igloo-shaped stone shepherds' shelter here, bearing a plaque that commemorates bravery during the Second World War. Our track divides at this shelter; take the right-hand fork and walk a further 150m/yds to the refuge, reached in 1h.

The return follows the same route.

21 THE SAMARIA GORGE

See also photographs pages 23, 95, 110
Distance: 18km/11.2mi; 4-6h
Open: April/May to October (depending on rainfall); there is a charge to enter; pick up an English leaflet on payment.
Grade: strenuous, particularly if you are not used to walking; the descent is 1300m/4300ft.
Equipment: stout shoes or walking boots, sunhat, water bottle (in which to collect spring water), picnic, swimming things
How to get there: 🚌 to Omalos (Timetable 3); journey time about 45min (get off at the last stop, Xiloskala).
To return: 🚢 to Hora Sfakion, departs Agia Roumeli 15.45, 16.30, 17.00, 17.45; voyage time 1h30min. Then 🚌 from Hora Sfakion (Timetable 4); journey time about 2h

The Samaria Gorge may be one of the reasons why you have come to Crete. Even if it isn't, you will soon hear tell of it; few people can resist the lure of Europe's longest gorge. And you won't be disappointed. But although this walk follows a well-trodden path, walking the gorge requires some stamina and robust footwear is essential.

Enough about caution. Here's some scene-setting: the landscape is simply spectacular, from the top of the gorge at Omalos to the bottom at Agia Roumeli — and all along the south coast on your boat trip to Hora Sfakion (where you'll find your bus back to Hania and the north coast). The White Mountains tower around you as the route leads seawards under shady pine trees through which sunlight slants. You'll pass cool pools and cross wide-open stretches of ancient, bleached rocky riverbed. Imagine light and shadow; height and depth; rock in shades of grey, green, blue and brown; mountains, trees and sky;

In the height of summer this can look like a bridge to nowhere, without the torrents of spring coursing below it.

birdsong and silence. It's a special experience walking through this natural wonder. If you walk the gorge in springtime, the wild flowers are another bonus to the excursion. At whatever time of year you walk the gorge, don't go down helter-skelter, trying to beat any records. Go at a leisurely pace and take in your surroundings. We haven't given any times for reaching specific points on the walk for this very reason. Enjoy the day.

Important note: Do not try to find an alternative route to the sea; stay on the designated path through the gorge. *This is imperative.* Swimming in the rock pools is forbidden; console yourself with the thought of a swim at the end of the walk.

The bus drops you by two cafeneions (with shops and WC), where you can re-organise yourselves before starting out. **The walk starts** on the 'xiloskala', the wooden staircase down into the gorge. This is a well-devised, solid construction made of tree trunks. Before setting out, you will purchase a ticket; hang on to it. Half of it will be taken from you at the end of the gorge; it helps wardens to ascertain if everyone has gone through the gorge at the end of the day and, of course, it aids 'statistics'. Doubtless there will be a mass of other people setting off with you, which isn't encouraging, but the crowd thins out as people establish their individual pace and walk and stop and walk again, marvelling at this splendid achievement of nature.

The first eye-catcher is Gingilos Mountain (see photograph on page 95) — a huge wall of rock towering majestically up to the right. You may well have already climbed Gingilos at our suggestion (Walk 19), before descending into the gorge; it's a tremendous feeling to see the mountain from here, particularly if you have been to the top …

The staircase becomes a path and drops down a staggering 1000m/3280ft to the bottom of the upper gorge — in just the first two kilometres of the walk. There are springs and drinking troughs and a couple of WCs en route. Once you've passed the small chapel of Agios Nikolaos, nestling amongst pines and cypresses to the right, the route becomes less steep. When you reach the old hamlet of Samaria you will be about halfway to the sea. Lots of people make use of the benches and tables to enjoy a picnic here, although there are masses of other delightful and quiet spots along the way. One of the buildings (into which you can go and sign the visitors' book) has been

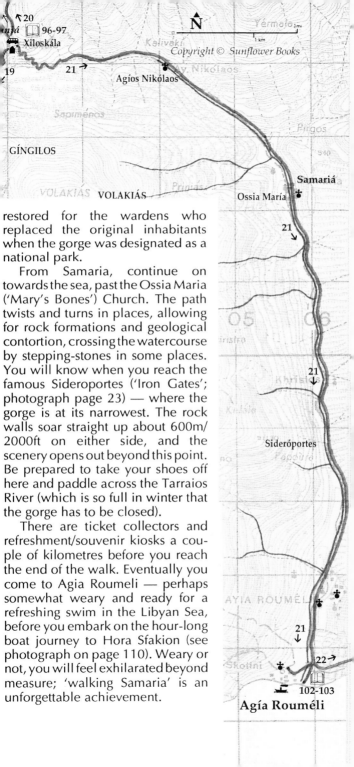

N

Copyright © Sunflower Books

restored for the wardens who replaced the original inhabitants when the gorge was designated as a national park.

From Samaria, continue on towards the sea, past the Ossia Maria ('Mary's Bones') Church. The path twists and turns in places, allowing for rock formations and geological contortion, crossing the watercourse by stepping-stones in some places. You will know when you reach the famous Sideroportes ('Iron Gates'; photograph page 23) — where the gorge is at its narrowest. The rock walls soar straight up about 600m/ 2000ft on either side, and the scenery opens out beyond this point. Be prepared to take your shoes off here and paddle across the Tarraios River (which is so full in winter that the gorge has to be closed).

There are ticket collectors and refreshment/souvenir kiosks a couple of kilometres before you reach the end of the walk. Eventually you come to Agia Roumeli — perhaps somewhat weary and ready for a refreshing swim in the Libyan Sea, before you embark on the hour-long boat journey to Hora Sfakion (see photograph on page 110). Weary or not, you will feel exhilarated beyond measure; 'walking Samaria' is an unforgettable achievement.

22 FROM AGIA ROUMELI TO LOUTRO

Map continues on page 106; see also cover photograph

Distance: 15km/9.3mi; 4h35min

Grade: moderate to strenuous, with some scrambling, but no appreciable climbs or descents; E4-waymarked

Equipment: stout shoes, sunhat, picnic, water, swimming things

How to get there: 🚌 to Hora Sfakion (Timetable 4); journey time about 2h. Then 🚢 to Agia Roumeli: departs Hora Sfakion 09.30, 10.15, 11.00, 15.30, 17.00; voyage time 1h30min

To return: 🚢 from Loutro to Hora Sfakion: departs 16.30, 17.45; voyage time 30min. Then 🚌 to Hania (Timetable 4); journey time about 2h

Alternative walks: Combine this with walk 21, 23 or 24.

The gorgeous sea walk from Agia Roumeli to Hora Sfakion splits comfortably and conveniently into two parts, and that's how we describe it. But whether you undertake it as one walk or two, do start out early, to benefit from the early morning cool and the sunrise.

The first stage of the walk has ample shade, but the leg from Loutro to Hora Sfakion is virtually devoid of it. High cliffs form a towering wall to the left, sometimes close at hand, edging the path, in other places set back in high majesty. Moving east, you will skirt or cross beaches, walk

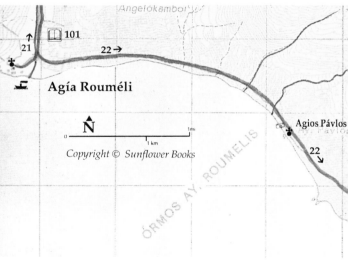

under pine trees — scrunching their needles and inhaling the heady scent, edge along high, but safe cliff paths, and scramble over boulders. With the sparkling sea hemming your route on the right all the way, you'll cover a great distance and have some lovely swimming opportunities. Agia Roumeli is a very pleasant place to stay overnight,

Take a break — or spend the night — at delightful Loutro.

after the Samaria Gorge-walkers have left with the last boat. The same is true of Loutro. Both have rooms for rent.

From the middle of Agia Roumeli, **start out** by walking between the Samaria Hotel and Tara Rooms for Rent — away from the sea and towards the bottom of the Samaria Gorge. At the edge of the village you will be on a rubble track. The track bends round, away from the village. The riverbed leading from the gorge is on your right. Cross over the riverbed — via stepping stones between an old bridge and the sea — picking up the waymarked path on the far side. The small church en route is Agios Pavlos (**1h25min**). Vertigo sufferers may find the going a bit testing at about the **3h40min**-point, where the high path edges the side of the cliff. As you approach Loutro there is a stunning view of the castle in its commanding position above the blue, blue sea. You enter the village in **4h35min**.

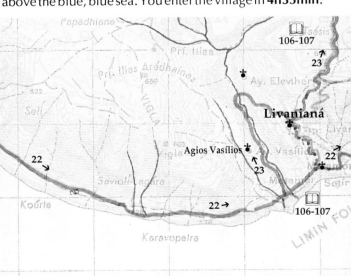

23 LOUTRO AND THE ARADHENA GORGE

See also cover photograph and photographs pages 31 and 103

Distance: 15km/9.3mi; 6h

Grade: straightforward, but involving 650m/2150ft of ascents/descents, some quite steep. You must be sure-footed and have a head for heights (possibility of vertigo). E4-waymarking on part of the route

Equipment: stout shoes, sunhat, picnic, water, swimming things

How to get there: 🚌 to Hora Sfakion (Timetable 4); journey time about 2h. Then ⛴ to Loutro: departs 10.30, 12.00, 14.00, 16.50, 18.15; voyage time 30min

To return: ⛴ from Loutro to Hora Sfakion: departs 16.30, 17.45; voyage time 30min. Then 🚌 from Hora Sfakion: departs 30min after each boat arriving from Agia Roumeli.

Shorter walk: Loutro — Aradhena Gorge — Livaniana — Loutro 8km/5mi; 3h15min). Grade, equipment, access/return as main walk (but only half the climbing). Follow the main walk for 2h15min, to the outskirts of Livaniana. Instead of turning sharply left here, descend through the houses of Livaniana. By the last few houses in the lower part of the village, you reach a track. Follow it down the hillside to the Phoenix tavernas, then retrace your outgoing route back to Loutro.

Alternative walks: Start out by descending the Samaria Gorge, then stay overnight at Agia Roumeli and/or Loutro, so that you can do Walks 22 and 24, as well as this walk.

This is a glorious combination of coast, seaside village, gorge and mountain village, which can be done either way round. We choose to walk two-thirds of the way up the gorge (enjoying the best part of it), and then *downhill back* to Loutro — since this section is long, steep and exposed. However, if you stay overnight in Loutro you will no doubt meet people who walk *up* to Anopolis, on to Aradhena, and *down* the gorge. This descent involves climbing 20 rungs down a steel ladder bolted to the rock-face — fine for the agile walker who does not suffer from vertigo, but it's no place to lose your footing.

Start the walk at Loutro's harbour. Coming from the concrete boat jetty, look between two tavernas (to the left of ΜΑΔΑΡΕΣ taverna), up some steps, for a sign directing you to 'Phonix'. Climb up; the path zigzags steeply up the hillside, heading west out of Loutro. At the top of the path, turn right following more signs for Phoenix, and cross a flat rocky area. To the left Loutro's ruined castle rises on the headland. The path follows the wall surrounding these ruins and leads to the brow of the hillside. The village tucked up into the hillside ahead, to the right, is Livaniana, which is skirted later in the walk. Soon your complete coastal route can be seen stretching out in front of you.

As you start descending, Phoenix comes into view — a smattering of blue and white tavernas and rooms for rent. The route heads down behind them on a zigzag track. At the Phoenix sign, where there is also a prominent E4 sign, take the right-hand fork; the path heads behind the tavernas, leaving a whitewashed church with two palm trees down to the left. Just past the church, cross diagonally over a rough track waymarked with bright blue Δs which runs down from Livaniana (the return route for the Shorter walk). Continue on the well-waymarked (E4) path in the general direction of the coast, ignoring the Δs waymarking the track. Before long you are over the next small headland (where there are more tavernas with rooms to rent) and down by the sea; this is Likkos.

Keep straight on downhill, hugging the rocks on your left. Descend amidst the line of buildings (**30min**). The path heads down some concrete steps, across taverna terraces, and then across a flat pebbly stretch behind a

The old church at Aradhena, rising above the gorge

beach. The last building en route is a restaurant. Walk along this beach to the next cove, at the far side of which there is an E4 sign. Here steps hewn out of the rock take you steeply up onto the cliffs. You need to walk carefully here, as the path curls tightly up to the right, past a cave. Where the path is difficult to discern yellow paint daubs identify the route. Those who suffer from vertigo will find this the most difficult part of the walk. Once over the next headland you will be looking down over Marmara ('Marble') Beach, beyond which are a few buildings and a small church. The path descends to a flatter area and bears left to the beach (**1h15min**). The water is crystal clear and very inviting.

From here *ignore* the E4 signs, which now lead along the coast. Instead, head inland, following a streambed into the mouth of the Aradhena Gorge. The atmosphere changes rapidly as huge rock faces tower either side of the route, providing cooling shade. Five minutes into the gorge, the magnificent rock wall on your right has a cave at its base. Follow the twists and turns of the streambed. By **1h25min** it looks as if a massive boulder blocks the way — perhaps it's the 'plug' that has come out of the mountainside above and ahead, leaving a cave? Follow red and blue waymarking to the right of the boulder, scrambling over a huge rockfall for five minutes. Then, to get back down to the streambed, head towards the left-hand rock wall. Cairns will show you the way back to the

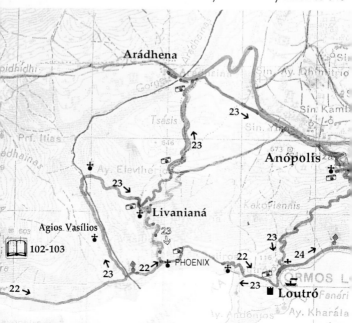

streambed, where you pick up the red waymarking again. Continue on through a thicket of bushes. At **1h35min** waymarking will direct you around another rockfall, as you climb more steeply.

At **1h40min** a water trough and a large oleander bush make a peaceful resting spot in amongst the rocks. Beyond here, look for waymarking on the left-hand side of the gorge, pointing uphill, away from the trough, and taking you into another scramble. Follow the waymarking carefully — it's very precise! Five minutes from the water trough the path flattens out, and the landscape opens up. A boulder with red, yellow and blue paint marks comes into sight on the left. Follow the yellow arrow indicating Livaniana — to the right. You skirt round a large olive tree, as you climb up the right-hand side of the gorge. Yellow waymarking gives way to blue as the path winds up the hillside through old terraced olive trees towards the rock face on your right.

Having hugged the rock face, the steep path comes up to a chicken-wire-topped, walled enclosure; keep it close by on your right and continue uphill through more terracing. Then turn right through a gap in the wall, between wooden gateposts (**2h10min**). Continue to follow the waymarking. A few minutes from the gateposts, the path turns left, following a stone wall. A minute later there is a wonderful view down over the coast, and Livaniana's church is just a few metres ahead of you (**2h15min**). This is the upper part of the almost-deserted village of Livaniana, and you are at a junction. *The Shorter walk goes straight ahead here, descending through Livaniana.*

The main walk turns *sharply left,* avoiding the village: walk between the wall with chicken wire on the left and the wire fence on the right — you will notice a red waymark. The rocky path climbs along the right-hand side of a wall; keep beside the wall. When the walled and fenced enclosure ends, the path continues straight ahead. At this point you reach a rocky outcrop and, continuing

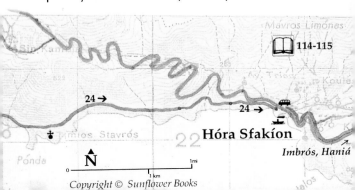

Copyright © *Sunflower Books*

along the ridge, you encounter another stone wall: keep this wall on your right and head across an open area; the sea is now in sight again. Ahead you can see the stone walls supporting your ongoing path, as it climbs the hillside.

At **2h35min** the path opens out on a flatter area; look carefully for the waymarking here — and later, as you start to climb again in zigzags. Watch for the eagles that are often seen here — it will help take your mind off the long haul — and they are likely to be breathtakingly close. A track/dirt road is visible ahead cutting across the hillside; the path joins it at just under the **3h**-mark, after a fairly steep climb. Turn left on this dirt road and follow it in a bend to the right. Although dirt roads usually make for a rather boring walk, this one affords magnificent views over Livaniana and the beaches below — you can see Likkos, Phoenix and part of Loutro. Follow the road over the hill and onto a plateau.

Eighteen minutes from where the path met this road you round a bend and have a wonderful view of the White Mountains ... marred only by a concrete animal shed in the foreground. Pass this shed, ignoring a fork off to the right just before it. Ten minutes later the road has turned away from the coast, behind the shed, and you are heading straight towards the mountains. Barren, rock-strewn grazing land and animal enclosures lie off to the left.

The houses and old church of Aradhena come into sight (**3h45min**). Walk towards the church and, just as you reach a T-junction, you will see to the left an iron bridge that gives access to the village; the photograph on page 105 was taken from this point. (It's worth turning left and making a detour into the village which, although mostly deserted, has signs of renovation. Until 1986 Aradhena was only approachable by the steep donkey path visible down the sides of the gorge below. The churchyard makes a pleasant shaded place to sit. We have not included the time for this detour in our notes.)

The main walk heads right at the T-junction. After three minutes, just before a stone wall, head right on a track, passing under power cables. After about 50 paces look carefully on the left for a cairn, placed almost directly below the power cables, just before a wall on which there are red waymarks. Follow the wall, and fork left under an ancient olive tree. You are now on a rough old cobbled path. Fifteen minutes from the T-junction the houses of Anopolis (still spelled with an 's' at the end, but pronounced Anopoli) come into view. At about this point the cobbles run out abruptly, but the waymarked path is clear as it heads downhill. Follow it between stone walls and turn left. Then, almost immediately (where the path meets a fence), walk left towards the houses of Anopolis. The path continues past houses on the right; a stone wall is on the left. At the next T-junction, where steps go up to the left, turn right on concrete; the edge of the village and the mountains are straight ahead. Pass the small chapel shown on page 31, on the left and surrounded by lovely shady holm oaks, and then turn right on an asphalt road. The village sign is along the road to the left.

After 15 minutes on this road, at a T-junction (where there is a taverna on the left), turn right to reach the village 'square' in Anopolis (**4h20min**). It is more of a circle, with a statue of Daskalogiannis in the middle. Head right and look for a sign up on a wall: 'Loutro No Car'. Follow this road. Asphalt gives way to concrete almost as soon as you come to the edge of the village square. Passing through the last houses, the track goes into a hairpin bend. Here take another track going off to the left. Just 10m/yds past here, you can take a footpath off right, to cut a bend off the track. Having climbed up between some houses, come back to the track and turn left, to follow the track seawards. There's a nice view looking back over the fertile plain around Anopolis.

Some 25 minutes from the square, when the track ends at a flat area, walk right towards a shrine. The path straight ahead here goes down to Loutro, 1h15min away. First, however, for an even more fantastic view and a very worthwhile 15 minute detour, head steeply up to the right from the shrine, to a church with a fine viewing platform. Then return to the path and descend *carefully* to Loutro; this path (see cover photograph) requires steady footwork. Ten minutes from the shrine ignore a path forking left, back to Anopolis. Some minutes later, pass a water cistern and join a bulldozed track. Head down to the right and after about 100m/yds cairns on the left signal where you rejoin the path. When you next meet the track, more cairns point the way (straight over). The path crosses a gulley. Some 25 minutes later you come to a fork: the right fork goes to 'Finix'. Take the *left* fork, down to Loutro. Fifteen minutes later pass a shrine on the left (where Walk 24 begins) and head right, towards the village. Clamber through a stock control gate and in five minutes (**6h**) you're back where you started — more than ready for a swim.

24 FROM LOUTRO TO HORA SFAKION

See map pages 106-107; see also photographs page 103 and cover
Distance: 6km/3.7mi; 2h
Grade: strenuous, with some scrambling (although there are no appreciable climbs/descents); you must be sure-footed and have a head for heights (possibility of vertigo). E4-waymarked. *Very little shade en route*
Equipment: stout shoes, sunhat, picnic, water, swimming things
How to get there: 🚌 to Hora Sfakion (Timetable 4); journey time about 2h. Then 🚢 to Loutro: departs 09.30, 10.15, 11.00, 15.30, 17.00; voyage time 30min
To return: 🚌 from Hora Sfakion (Timetable 4; as above)
Alternative walk: Tack this on to Walk 22 (6h35min) — or stay overnight in the area to explore Walks 21 and 23 as well.

Loutro is a wonderful, away-from-it-all backwater, perfect for really relaxing — particularly as there is no traffic, bar boats. From the ferry you will see the route heading east along the hillside above the coast.

To start the walk head up from the harbour to the left of the Taverna Kri-kri, at the east end of the bay. The coastal path starts at an easily-visible shrine. (Walk 23 comes directly down the hillside in zigzags to this point.) Those who suffer from vertigo may experience difficulty in **15min** (where the path runs near the cliff-edge, with a steep drop down to the sea), and again at the **30min**-point (where the path crosses a stretch of sandy scree). Some **1h20min** from Loutro (about 40 minutes short of Hora Sfakion), the path runs perhaps 70m/200ft or more above the sea, and there is a sheer drop down to the right. This stretch lasts for 10-12 minutes.

When the path meets asphalt road, on a bend, turn right and walk into Hora Sfakion (**2h**), where you can take a break before the bus ride back to Hania.

Hora Sfakion from the sea. There are regular sailings to Loutro, Agia Roumeli, Sougia and Paleohora.

25 THE IMBROS GORGE • KOMITADES • HORA SFAKION

See map pages 114-115; see photographs opposite and page 12

Distance: 11km/6.8mi; 3h50min

Grade: fairly straightforward descent of 600m/2000ft in a gorge

Equipment: stout shoes, sunhat, picnic, water, swimming things

How to get there: Hora Sfakion 🚌 to Imbros (Timetable 4); journey time about 1h45min. *Idea:* Sit on the left-hand side of the bus for best views. *To return:* 🚌 from Hora Sfakion to Hania (Timetable 4); journey time 1h45min

Shorter walk: Imbros Gorge — Komitades (7km/4.3mi; 2h50min). Grade, equipment, access as main walk. Follow the main walk to Komitades and from there take a 🚌 to Hora Sfakion Timetable 16): departs Komitades about 15.30-16.00; journey time 10min. Then 🚌 as above.

This is a really delightful amble through the peace and quiet of pines in the Imbros Gorge, which narrows and widens in places very dramatically — until you reach the south coast and the Libyan Sea. The bus rides are quite long, since you follow a winding route from the north to south coast and then back again, but these journeys enable you to see a good slice of Cretan countryside.

The bus will drop you in the village of Imbros. **Start out** by walking south, in the same direction as the bus is continuing. At the end of the village, just by a shrine on the left-hand side of the road, turn down hard left onto a track. This track leads away from the village and becomes a footpath as it meets the streambed. The stream — when it flowed — would have coursed its way to the sea from here, via the gorge. Once you are on the route, it's virtually impossible to lose your way.

Turn right and very soon you will be in the gorge itself, surrounded by Jerusalem sage, striking in spring and early summer. The route leads all the way to the coast; sometimes the path is in the gorge, sometimes it runs beside it to avoid large boulders. Anywhere around here is a good place to picnic (Picnic 25; photograph page 12). By **50min** into the walk, you will be briefly on a donkey trail. After **1h30min** of easy walking you will pass an animal shelter and water trough (in summer, you may find an enterprising young man here selling drinks). At **2h20min** you can see the south coast and the sea ahead in the middle distance. You should just be able to make out the 14th-century Venetian fort, Frangokastello.

By **2h30min** the countryside has opened out and, looking to the right, you will see a faded waymark arrow by a path bordered by stone walls. Follow the path which will take you to the main road. The village off to the left is Vraskas. Step down onto the road and turn right. Walk on to the village ahead, Komitades (**2h50min**). Either wait here for a bus (Shorter walk) or continue to Hora Sfakion, an hour away. To continue to Hora Sfakion, keep on the road and, 10 minutes later (where you join the main Hora Sfakion road at a T-junction), turn left. You can wait for the Hania bus here but, if it is full, it may not stop. By **3h50min** you're in the centre of Hora Sfakion, its small harbour bristling with cafeneions and tavernas.

26 ASKYFOU • ASFENDOS • AGIOS NEKTARIOS

See photograph opposite   **Distance:** 15km/9.3mi; 5h15min
Grade: moderate, with an ascent of about 400m/1300ft and descent of 950m/3100ft, the latter part in a gorge
Equipment: stout shoes, sunhat, picnic, water
How to get there: Hora Sfakion 🚌 to Kares (Timetable 4); journey time about 1h20min
To return: 🚌 from Agios Nektarios to Hora Sfakion (not in the timetables, but departs 16.00 daily); journey time 20 minutes. Then 🚌 to Hania (Timetable 4); journey time about 2h

One of our favourite walks, this excursion combines a good bus ride, covering masses of ground, with a walk across the lovely plain shown opposite and then over some easy mountain terrain. We finish with a descent through a gorge, with the Libyan Sea as our goal. The road that the bus follows is the route along which thousands of war-weary soldiers trudged in 1941, when they withdrew, under relentless air attack, to the south coast. The walk leads you through a gorgeous chunk of Cretan countryside — spectacular anytime, but particularly picturesque in spring, when the plain at Askyfou is dotted with poppies and the gorge is lined with bright yellow Jerusalem sage.

Be ready to get off the bus when, having wound up and round hillsides, you see the Askyfou plain come into sight below left. Before you leave the bus, it passes an eye-catching old Turkish fort, strategically positioned on a hillock mid-plain. Then the bus passes the sign denoting the boundary of Askyfou village. You will be dropped at a junction and the bus will go straight on.

Start out by crossing the main road and taking the turn left off the road. You head south, down towards a hamlet and the plain below it. At the next junction you will be in the hamlet of Kares; turn left on a concrete track. The track forks by a telephone pole, where there is a walnut tree on the corner (**10min**): go off left. This route will take you across the plain itself, via fields of vegetables planted and tended by the Askyfou villagers. Within a few minutes, ignore a rough stone track going left (the track you are on also becomes stony). Pass a well, also on your left. Soon, at the next cross-tracks, turn left and head in the direction of the Turkish fort.

By **20min** into the walk, you meet an asphalt road: go

Left: looking westwards towards the White Mountains, from the poppy-bright plain of Askyfou (Walk 26).

left. A church, its graveyard surrounded by the customary cypress trees, lies to the left. The road rises as you approach Seli, the next village, and a concrete track takes you round to the right. The track skirts the village and ends by an old building with 'No. 20' painted on it and double metal doors. Take the earthen track straight ahead, to the right of the building. Stay on the track as it bends round and away from Seli, with the wonderful views shown on page 112. Continue straight on, ignoring a grass track to the right and another to the left. Seli is directly behind you now.

Keep going until the track forks at a T-junction (**1h**). Go left, as indicated by a red arrow; 'Asfendos' is written in Greek on a boulder. After several minutes uphill, leave the track and take a path going off left (**1h10min**). Stay with the waymarking. The path climbs until, at **1h30min**, it levels out on an open grassy area. Seven minutes later the path divides; go left (red arrow). Ahead on the hillside notice some stone walls that underpin the ongoing path. Aiming for those walls, follow the path past a water trough and under two large hollyoak trees. The way leads up and continues to the left on the stone-built section ahead. The footpath widens out on the walls, which zigzag up to the top of the rise.

Now, at **1h45min**, a well-established path gradually starts the descent to the sea. It obviously took a lot of work to create this path. Keep on downhill; the route leads across another open grassy area, past an animal shelter and a group of trees set off to the left. Reaching the far side of the flat grazing land, you will catch sight of the distant sea for the first time. A stony track leads off from here. You can take the path which goes off to the right of the track. It descends, meeting the track again after 10 minutes. Cross the track and look for the rather indistinct path again. (It's worth taking the path as it is more direct and cuts some loops off the track.) At **2h25min** pass a reservoir on the left, and stay on the track. Be aware that you are heading for the V of the gorge ahead.

Still on track, as you round a bend, the very basic houses of Asfendos come into sight (**2h40min**). The village church is high up on the right. A few minutes later you come to a wire mesh animal gate; go through and turn left on another rubble track. Then, on the first bend (where there is a house high up on the left), take the rough track

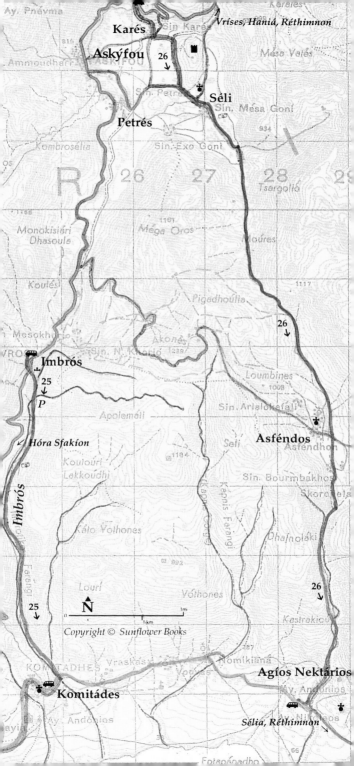

that leads right off the main track. Leave Asfendos and take the rocky path that heads left off the track almost immediately. For seven minutes or so there are walls either side of the path, which show evidence of past waymarking.

Keep straight downhill, ignoring paths off left or right, and make sure you have walls either side of you at first, and then on at least one side or the other. The V becomes a U in the distance, the left-hand side of it opening outwards as you near the gorge. The path is thickly edged with Jerusalem sage — a glorious bright yellow mass in spring. About half an hour from Asfendos there are clear signs that part of this path was formerly paved. You can see the gorge clearly now, ahead of you. Forty minutes from Asfendos (**3h20min**), you will see the sea in the cleft ahead, and scree comes in on the right. Five minutes further on, pass a waymarked boulder. The path then does a double bend and zigzags down the hillside. Although you are high, the gorge is too layered to pose any problems for vertigo sufferers.

Keep on curving down the hillside amongst any goats and sheep that might be about. About 1h30min from Asfendos (**4h10min**) you will be able to see the beach and sea below and ahead of you. Ten minutes after spotting the beach, stay on the path that bends round to the left and snakes down the hill, ignoring a smaller path that leads across the side of the gorge. Your path curves round past a shepherds' hut with a metal door — built into the mountain — and, three minutes later, it passes across the bottom of an animal stockade. If you find any forks in the path, just continue in the same direction, down the side of the gorge. Before long, you will find that the route criss-crosses the dry riverbed. Ten minutes from the start of these riverbed crossings, you will be high above the dry riverbed again.

Some 2h20min from Asfendos (**5h**) the path divides; go right. After a few minutes a fence comes in from the right. The path comes down to a gravelly area, where there is a concrete building on the left. Walk past the building and then between the few houses of Agios Nektarios, to the south coast road. A church lies to the left.

Turn right on the main road and continue until you come — very shortly — to a cafeneion on the left (currently painted sludge green; **5h15min**). A bus for Hora Sfakion will pass at about 16.00; if you've missed it, you can telephone for a taxi at the cafeneion, or perhaps hitch a lift.

27 CIRCUIT VIA MONI PREVELI

Distance: 18km/11.2mi; 5h15min

Grade: easy-moderate, with ascents/descents of about 250m/800ft

Equipment: stout shoes, sunhat, picnic, water, swimming things, suitable dress for Moni Preveli (trousers for men, longish skirts for women)

How to get there: 🚌 to Rethimnon (Timetable 1); journey time 1h. Then Plakias 🚌 (Timetable 15) to Asomatos; journey time 35min. Recheck with the bus driver departure times for the return journey.

To return: 🚌 from Asomatos to Rethimnon (Timetable 15); journey time 35min. (The bus leaves Asomatos a few minutes after departure from Plakias.) Then 🚌 to Hania (Timetable 1); journey time 1h

Shorter walk: Asomatos — Moni Preveli (10km/6.2mi; 3h). Easy; generally a descent of 250m/800ft. Equipment and access as main walk. Follow the main walk to Moni Preveli, where you can catch a 🚌 to Rethimnon (Timetable 14; *summer only*); journey time 45min.

This is a beautiful circuit, but rather long. If you don't mind hitch-hiking or taking an extra bus, it can be cut short at various points should the heat prove too exhausting or the temptations of flopping on the beach too much.

The walk starts in the village of Asomatos which is perched near the start of the dramatic Kourtaliotiko Gorge. The bus drops you off in the centre of the village by the signposted junction to Moni Preveli (8km to the south). **To start off**, head back towards the gorge on the asphalt

road and, just before it bends sharp left into the gorge (**10min**), turn sharp right downhill on a concrete track. In about six minutes you come to a large prefab building housing a modern olive press on your left and a watermill on your right. Continue straight ahead on the now-rough track for another six minutes, until it bends sharply to the left. Here take a fairly indistinct track straight ahead, passing an old stone chapel on your right. Your route is now an overgrown but perfectly viable path. Follow it downhill, until you reach an abandoned olive press dating from 1890; its crumbling stone walls still provide enough shelter for it to be used as a stable (**30min**). For a perfect picnic spot, walk past the front of the mill and continue on a path through a meadow to the tree line beyond. Go left at the tree line and, after 20 paces or so, go down right to the Megalopotamos — one of the few rivers in Crete that flows all year round (Picnic 27).

Then return to the olive press/stable and head south-west on the dirt track (a continuation of the path you were on). A couple of minutes later, turn left on the asphalt road running parallel with the river. Within 10 minutes or so (**1h**) turn left and cross a steeply-arched early 19th-century bridge spanning the river. (There's a makeshift taverna here in summer.) Now follow the dirt track along the east side of the river, crossing another, cobbled bridge in 10 minutes, and continuing on the right-hand track.

About five minutes or so further on, a derelict monastery appears on your right: leave the track and go through a wire gate and past the chapel (the only building not in ruins), turning left into a very small olive grove. Some 40m/yds along, go through a fence and continue on a track that dips down into a gulley and climbs up the other side, continuing in a southerly direction above the river.

Within 400m/yds the track narrows into a path and the valley opens up; you can just see the walls of a narrow gorge ahead (**1h25min**). Occasional red waymarks confirm your route, and the path is well defined. Stay right when the path splits (**1h30min**), and keep right again just afterwards. After another 10 minutes, when you've climbed somewhat, make a short detour to the right, down to the edge of a narrow gorge: from here there is a fine view of the palm-lined river far below. Back on the main path, you pass under some electricity cables (**1h50min**). Just afterwards the Libyan Sea and Palm Beach at Preveli come into full view, looking *unbelievably* inviting.

Start the descent, following cairns and red waymarks (agility and surefootedness are required here). A large taverna (with road access) on the neighbouring beach to the east comes into view: you don't want to head in that direction, but you *do* want to join the path linking the two beaches. At the first T-junction turn left, away from Palm Beach; the path descends steeply, becoming indistinct in places — watch for cairns marking the way. When you come almost to the edge of the headland (30m/yds from a fence), be sure to turn right and look for cairns. Then, at a second T-junction, just before the sea, turn right onto the path

Left: Palm Beach (Preveli Beach), where the Megalopotamos River empties into the crystal-clear waters of the Libyan Sea. This palm-fringed oasis can be very crowded in high season, but it is still beautiful. Below: Moni Preveli

linking the two beaches. Five minutes later you arrive a
Palm Beach (**2h15min**). After a swim and a rest, wad
across the river to the far side of the beach (where there'
a cafe-bar serving cool drinks in summer) and start th
waymarked climb up the other side of the gorge.

Within about 20 minutes you emerge in a parking are
of sorts, beyond which there is a wide dirt track that skirt
round a fenced area.* To continue to Moni Preveli, turn
instead onto a minor track leading off left (due west) from
the parking area. You pass a small cylindrical structure
on your left and a shepherds' hut on your right, befor
emerging in a barren area where the track seems to dis
appear. Walk straight ahead up the slope and regain th
track (**2h45min**). Leave the track on the first sharp ben
to the right: take a path straight ahead. Within five minute
the path joins the main road and Moni Preveli comes int
view, 10 minutes away. You can fill up with water at th
monastery (**3h**) and have a wander round, if you have th
proper clothing with you. In *summer only*, you can catc
a bus back to Rethimnon here; it travels via Asomatos.

To continue, take the dirt track that starts uphill off th
'roundabout' in front of the monastery. You reach a saddl
in about 20 minutes (**3h20min**). In another quarter of a
hour you are just outside Yianniou. Take a sharp right o
another track that goes downhill about 70m/yds before
fountain/watering hole on your left (just before enterin
the village). Almost immediately you come to a T-junctio
by a white-washed church: turn right (a left leads bac
up into Yianniou). In five minutes the track bends round
to the left and passes another church (Agia Paraskevi) o
a ridge. Just after this church keep right downhill. Fiv
minutes later, turn left at a junction (a right also eventuall
leads down to the asphalt road). The track threads its wa
through some lovely countryside and meets the aspha
road. Turn left; the derelict monastery of Kato ('lower
Preveli will be on the right. This original 'Moni Prevel
was abandoned at the time of the Ottoman conquest.

Continue on the asphalt road for 10 minutes, until yo
reach the steeply-arched bridge you crossed about a
hour into the walk (**4h15min**). To get back to Asomato
from here you can either retrace your footsteps, or kee
to the asphalt road, turning right at the next T-junctio
It's about an hour's walk either way (**5h15min**). Hitch
hiking this last stretch should not prove too difficult.

*At press date there was a fenced area, in which trees were being plante
as part of a project to turn the whole area into a national park.

See also photograph page 125 **Distance:** 8km/5mi; 4h20min

Grade: fairly strenuous ascent and descent of 550m/1800ft. The final ascent is not waymarked and involves some clambering; you must be sure-footed.

Equipment: stout shoes, long socks/trousers in spring, sunhat, picnic, water

How to get there and return: 🚌 to/from Ano Meros: park in the main street, near the church. If friends can take you to or collect you from Ano Meros, you might use a 🚐 in one direction (not in the timetables; journey 1h30min): departs Rethimnon 14.30; departs Ano Meros 16.00.

Note: If you are driving, watch for the monastery shown on pages 34-35 (Agios Ioannis Theologos); it is on the left-hand side of the road, between Gerakari and Ano Meros, with parking opposite.

Kedros is the elongated mountain on the western side of the Amari Valley, rising to 1775m/5800ft. This walk takes you up its flanks to a viewpoint on a lesser peak, Tripiti, from where you will enjoy a tremendous outlook. Walk 29 surveys the valley from the flanks of Psiloritis, the huge mass facing Kedros from the east.

On the ascent and descent from Tripiti, your views encompass Mt Samitos and a reservoir in the Ligiotis Valley.

Start out by leaving the church of Ano Meros on your right: head south on the road. Immediately you enjoy the fantastic outlook towards Psiloritis shown on page 125. Fourfouras (Walk 29) lies below in the valley. Ignore the first small, stepped turning (Odos Markou Botsari) off to the right. Take the *next* right turn — a stepped concrete track. At the top of the flight of steps turn left; then, almost immediately, go right. The concrete track rises steeply, turns into rubble at the edge of the village, and then continues as a footpath running beside a water channel.

In **8min** meet a gravel track and turn right. Two minutes later stay on the main track, leaving another track off to the left. Head towards the mountains; there is a valley down to the right. In places you will see vestiges of old water channelling down the middle of the track. At **20min** fork off right to see the ruined chapel of Kaloidhena — part of a monastery destroyed by the Turks in 1821. The chapel, with its splendid view, is above a gated shady concrete picnic area, where a clear spring gushes by the gate. Steps lead up to the chapel, little of which is intact, bar the bell. Looking out over the Amari Valley you can still see part of the Platis River.

To continue the walk head back to the fork in the track and head up to the left. At the next T-junction go left, leaving an old ruined building up to your right. There are the remains of an old watermill down to the left just past the junction. In a few minutes go through a gateway and immediately go right in a tight U bend (there is a waymark on the rock ahead). Within 50m/yds the track seems to run out: here take a path going up to the left (trousers or long socks will come in handy now). The path curves round left at the end of a walled vineyard. Near some fencing, the path forks; go right. The path becomes clearer as you climb.

Very shortly cross over a rubble track where, looking up, you will see cairns straight ahead. The route is very sparsely waymarked with cairns, but keep it in mind that you want to climb onto and over the ridge ahead. When you join a track on that ridge, *take note of the spot* so that you can pick it up on your return. Turn right on the track. You can either keep to the track if you prefer easier going under foot, or leave the track after some 50-60m/yds, where you see the cairned path continuing down to the left. We prefer to keep to the footpath for a while. At this point it's also worth noting a square-cornered gap ahead, high in the mountainside — that's where we're going!

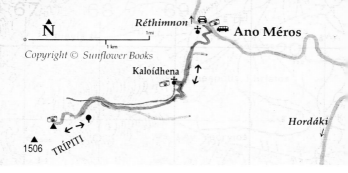

The path is waymarked with occasional red marks; it follows a water pipe. Where it forks and seems to run in parallel strands, keep heading for the square-cornered gap. Our route stays by the water pipe, arriving at an open water channel and a concreted well. Walk along the channel until you come to a group of mature trees — chestnut and almond. In front of the trees, across the water channel, follow the waymarking which leads sharply uphill. When the track again crosses your way, turn left on it; then, around the next bend, head left on your path. This is another case of a track ruining a pleasant path, as, five minutes later, you will have to join the track. As you look up at the square-cornered gap, you will be aware of an animal stockade below it, in a bluff of rock.

In **2h** we reach the top of the ridge; the track ends at a corrie where animals gather and shelter. Up to the left of the corrie is a smelly cave! If a mist has descended it is *not* advisable to climb beyond this point because there is no waymarking. Hopefully conditions will allow you to press on to a more inviting goal.

With your back to the cave, walk left, and curve hard round, as if you were going behind it. Cross over a low rock wall and then clamber over the rocks to your left, heading up towards a lone holly oak tree. Walk to the right of that tree, down over a small plateau/grazing area. From here you can see a concrete pillar up on the peak. It looks a long way off but it only takes about 20 minutes to get there (**2h20min**). Make your own way; just scramble up to it. Once there, you can look out over the Mesara Plain — where Festos and Agia Triada are sited — and across to the little island of Paximadia, just off the coast. The peninsula that juts out into the sea from Agia Galini is also visible in the distance.

Retrace your steps from here to Anos Meros (**4h20min**). Be sure to pick up the path at the place where you left it (the continuing track goes in a different direction altogether).

Distance: 12km/7.5mi; 5h45min

Grade: strenuous climb and descent of about 900m/3000ft. The paths are faint; much of the time you will be making your own way.

Equipment: walking boots, anorak, sunhat, compass, picnic, water

How to get there and return: 🚌 to/from Rethimnon (Timetable 1); journey time 1h. Then 🚌 to/from Fourfouras (not in the timetables, departs Rethimnon 07.00, 14.00 Mon-Sat; 14.00 Sun; departs Fourfouras 07.15, 15.00 Mon-Fri; 09.00, 16.15 Sat; 15.20 Sun); journey time 1h15min. Or 🚗 to/from Fourfouras.

It's hard to imagine the grand Psiloritis and the beautiful Amari Valley playing major roles in the Second World War, but they did, being the backdrop for many daring, courageous Resistance efforts. This walk makes a good day's hike to a trig point, Leska, where you can survey the scene above and below, contemplate the present and imagine the past. It's an uphill climb in no uncertain terms, and the constraints of bus times mean that you have to keep moving. (It's worth considering a taxi ride back to Rethimnon to save rushing.) You will want to take your time — both because the area is historically interesting and because the route is not always very obvious.

The bus stops by a petrol station on the outskirts of Fourfouras. The rounded mountain in the middle of the valley is Samitos. The higher, longer one behind it is Kedros (Walk 28). Both are more comfortable shapes than the challenging mountainside we tackle on this hike! Look behind the petrol station and notice the jagged peaks on the lower right-hand side of Psiloritis. That's where we're going! Beyond their fringe, the slopes of this great mountain change texture and colour.

Start out by walking back in the direction the bus came. Take the first, concrete track leading off right, heading in the direction of the mountains. Almost immediately, in about 30m/yds, at a fork, go right again. Then, at the next fork (60m/yds further on) bear right again on a dirt/gravel track (the concrete track continues off to the left). Keep going until you pass a huge concreted football ground (**13min**). Then, immediately, at the first T-junction, turn sharp right uphill. Follow the track in a fork round to the left; it may be necessary to negotiate a stock control gate (**25min**). If there is a gate, leave it as you find it. Continue on towards the mountain, now not quite so out of reach. The track bends firmly to the right; shortly beyond this bend, leave the track: a cairn indicates a footpath heading off left, up an embankment. Ahead of you at this point are three rocky outcrops that look like giant molars.

The climb starts here (**35min**). The path passes to the right of the 'molars' and meets the mouth of a ravine etched deep into the mountainside. You will see a distinct holly oak tree standing on its own. *Ignore* a cairn (if you even see it) about ten paces beyond the tree and take the next turn-off, some fifty paces from the tree. This leads you to the path between the rock spine and the ravine. Although not well defined at this stage, the path becomes a lot better and more visible once you have started climbing a bit — after, say, 50m/yds. Look out, too, for a distinctive rock on the route, shaped like a large beast — just beyond it there is a lovely panoramic view down over Fourfouras and across to Kedros. On a clear day it's possible to see Crete's south coast from up here, even though you have still got a fair climb to Leska; imagine what the view will be like when you get there!

The path becomes narrow and very steep (**1h05min**) and soon you will notice an outcrop of rock on the left, with a holly oak tree sprouting from three separate trunks. Beyond this tree you can see for miles over the northern reaches of the Amari Valley. Thirty paces after this outcrop the path forks. Go right uphill (the left-hand, lower fork follows a water pipe). There is no clear waymarking or defined path now, and you have to make your own way, aiming slightly to the right of the next rocky outcrop. When

From the cafeneion at Ano Meros, where Walk 28 starts, you look out over Fourfouras and up to Psiloritis (Mount Ida). This walk takes us into the lower foothills — the jagged peaks below Psiloritis.

the route reaches the rocky outcrop and surrounding trees
(**1h30min**), head right, continuing on a fairly narrow shelf
between rock on the left and tree-lined cleft on the right
(vertigo sufferers might have a moment of anxiety; **1h
35min**). Cross the beginning or top of the cleft and continue up and to the right, until you reach a lone holly oak
tree (**1h50min**). The edge of the big ravine comes into
view beyond this tree to the right as you look up; this is
a good place to break for a picnic.

Just over **2h** from the start of the walk, you will be in
another distinct wooded area of holly oaks and pines that
form a sheltered area for flocks. There's an outcrop of
startling boulders in the middle of it and some shepherds'
ruined dwellings. With the shepherds' hut on your right,
look upwards to see two holly oak trees — one on each
side of a boulder on which there is a prominent white
splodge: it looks like a waymark but is in fact only lichen.
Pass between the two trees and continue up on a path
that veers right, roughly aiming towards the right-hand
side of the orange-tinted rock face above. The path bends
uphill from here, following the edge of the ravine. You
reach another, flatter, more thickly-wooded and sheltered
grazing area for flocks (**2h30min**). In the middle of the
thickly-wooded area there is a large squat boulder:
20m/yds to the right of it (as you look up the hill) there is
a pinkish-coloured rocky outcrop. To the left of this
outcrop there's another big boulder: follow an ill-defined
path to the left of this boulder. You climb straight up the
hill, emerging between two very tall rocks, which together
form a U. As you continue up towards the ridge, look to
the left — to a huge isolated 'thumb' of rock (**2h37min**).
The path climbs roughly in that direction. To the left of
the 'thumb' there are some smaller boulders. Leave these
boulders about 50m/yds off to your right; make your way
uphill keeping close to the spine on the left.

Reach a saddle with views to the northern valley (**3h**).
Beyond here the going is far easier, and it's not much
further to the trig point and the wonderful view at the top
of Leska (**3h15min**). There's a shepherd's stone shelter
and a newer stone building up here as well. On the other
side of the peak, about 20m/yds downhill (on a plateau
called Korakia), you'll see a new track which leads down
to the neighbouring village of Vistayi.

Head back down to Fourfouras; it's a bit easier to make
out the way on the return trip. You should be back at the
petrol station in about 2h30min (**5h45min**).

30 THE KAMARES CAVE

Distance: 10km/6.2mi; 5h10min

Grade: a strenuous climb and descent of 950m/3100ft; you must be sure-footed and agile. E4 waymarked; plenty of water en route

Equipment: stout shoes, sunhat, water container, torch, picnic

How to get there and return: 🚗 to/from Kamares. (There is also a 🚌 from Rethimnon on Mondays-Fridays (Timetable 19), but timings are too tight to complete the walk.

This is somewhat of an aerobic exercise to a huge cave where the original cache of elaborate pottery known as Kamares Ware was found; it is now on display in the museum in Iraklion. The splendid cave, with a mouth 42m wide and 19m high (135ft x 62ft), is large and explorable. If you go to the back, and left of centre, search carefully and you will find the opening down on the floor, about 5m/15ft wide, where the pottery was found, in a fissure. For experienced climbers and walkers with the appropriate gear, Kamares is a good starting/finishing point for expeditions to the Nidha Plateau and Psiloritis.

Leave your car down off the main road, outside the church in Kamares village. **Start the walk** by heading east through the village. There's one of several pleasant old cafeneions just along on the left from the church. At the first fork, where there is a telegraph pole in the middle, keep straight on uphill (ignore Odos Ay Georgiou going off to the right). Within a few moments, at a three-way junction, stay on asphalt, forking left up 25th March Street.

At the top of the hill you meet the main road; a sign on the corner points onwards to the Cave of Kamares. Cross straight over, onto an old concreted road. After a five-minute pull uphill the concrete ends, and rough track continues. Look up to the right and notice the first E4 signpost. The path starts just beyond it, turning hard back off the track; be sure to turn right here (don't go ahead towards the water tank). The path turns steeply uphill, and the next E4 mark is on a tree. Old red waymarking is also visible before long. Soon after the tree the path turns left and a water culvert starts on the right. This water accompanies you most of the way uphill, in culverts or gulleys, providing good drinking opportunities from several troughs.

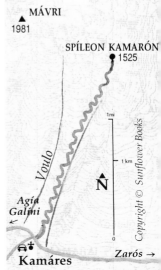

127

The path meets the end of a track (**15min**); walk to the left and pick up the path again going up to the right, at the end of some animal drinking wells. The path turns right and forks just after an E4 point; crossing the hillside, look for cairns to be sure of the route. Five minutes later there is a fantastic view as the path approaches the edge of a ravine. From the viewpoint the way heads back in the direction from which you've been coming and within three minutes you will be at a trough where fresh water pours in off the mountainside.

In **1h15min**, as you climb into a band of trees, cairn waymarking starts. Ten minutes later, look left for a place to cut through the trees and climb up onto a rock for a very good view into the Voulo ravine. The route flattens out, offering more views into the ravine. But before long the path is back in the trees and beginning to climb again. At **1h50min** there is another open trough with fresh water running into it. Continue beside the water gulley and soon see an E4 signpost pointing the way ahead. The next open water trough is ten minutes further up. The way appears to fork here in front of the trough; go right (east).

Beyond here the way is very steep and rough; you need to be sure-footed. Having swung round from the east and continued uphill — still guided by E4 signs — you will come to another water trough. Five minutes later, having struggled up to a concrete cistern, the path continues on up to the right — across the front of the cistern; here it is waymarked with red paint splodges. Fifteen minutes later the waymarks take you scrambling almost vertically up rocks. Five minutes later, look up — you will see the lip of the cave to the right of the path. As you approach the cave, several cairned routes lead towards it.

At a boulder marked with red arrows, the path forks (**2h35min**). Head left, towards two lone holly oak trees. In **3h** you will be at the top, in the cave's mouth — a pleasant place to relax before exploring the cave.

The return will be a bit quicker, and you should be back in Kamares village by **5h10min**.

Top: looking out from the cave's gigantic mouth; middle: approaching the cave; bottom: below the cave — the austere slopes of Psiloritis, dotted with holly oaks.

31 ELEFTHERNA

Distance: 7km/4.3mi; 1h45min (or up to 4h with diversions)
Grade: fairly easy ups and downs of about 100m/300ft, but some steep steps; a short part of the route is E4 waymarked
Equipment: stout shoes, sunhat, picnic, water, torch
How to get there and return: 🚌 to/from Rethimnon (Timetable 1); journey time 1h. Then 🚌 to/from Archaia Eleftherna (Timetable 18); journey time 1h. Or 🚗 to/from Archaia Eleftherna.

This is a short walk in a lush green valley of olive, orange, cypress and pine trees (ablaze with colourful wild flowers and cyclamen in spring). The spectacularly-sited Dorian city-state of Eleftherna (10th century BC) and a gem of a Hellenistic bridge are the main attractions. If you don't mind retracing your steps, the walk can be extended to four hours.

Start out in the centre of the Archaia Eleftherna: follow the road signposted to the Acropolis Taverna and site for 200m/yds. Then take the path immediately to the right of the taverna. In a minute you come to the Byzantine tower shown opposite; it rises on a north-pointing ridge between two streams, with steep drops on either side — an ideal defensive position for the ancient acropolis. This walk will take you to the bottom of the western valley (on your left as you face the tower), then north beyond where the two valleys meet, and back up the spine of the ridge.

Follow the ancient cobblestone path to the left of the tower (Picnic 31) and then go straight ahead for a few minutes, before making a sharp left turn downhill. (To the right, the smaller path continuing to the north is the one you'll be returning on at the end of the walk.) Immediately on your left, as you round the bend, you'll see a row of ancient rock-cut cisterns supported by massive stone columns. These cisterns are thought to be Roman or pre-Roman — well worth taking some time out to explore.

The path continues downhill, passing a sandstone cliff on the left and a (dry) spring with water troughs. A minute later you come to a T-junction, where a track goes off to the left. Here take the earthen trail to the right; it curves left and, in one minute, you reach another T-junction. Go right (north) on the path with the black-and-yellow (E4) waymark. *Keep careful watch* for your next turn-off: easily missed, it is on your left, about three minutes along — just where a stone wall begins on the right. (Some inconspicuous black-and-yellow waymarking and an E4 sign on a tree about 20m/yds *below* the fork mark the way; a small fenced archaeological dig lies to the left of the path a few minutes *past* your turn-off.)

Follow the black-and-yellow E4 waymarking down left to the streambed and up the other side of the valley. Ignore a path off to the right and go up some earthen steps. When you meet a track (**30min**), *don't* continue up the steps with the E4 waymarks; turn right on the track. Within a few minutes you'll see a concrete track on the right. This leads to the archaeological dig mentioned above, an interesting diversion (allow an *extra* 15 minutes return).

Continuing on, the track hairpins twice as it descends to the streambed, eventually crossing it over a small concrete water duct. About 25 paces on from here, look out for an ancient path climbing off to the right — your return route up the central ridge. For the moment, stay on the track which crosses another concrete duct, gradually climbing uphill. When the track bends sharply to the right, take the path dipping down to the left at the apex of this first bend (you may have to negotiate a wire gate). This steep and narrow path clings to a ledge on the eastern side of the valley, before descending to the streambed. Another fork in the path, a bit further on, also leads to the streambed: in spring, if the stream is too full of water, keep to this upper path.) By either route, you will come to a Hellenistic bridge (**1h**), one of the highlights of this walk and an ideal spot for a shady rest (Picnic 31).

From here continue up the path on the eastern side of the valley, until you emerge on an old, pleasantly overgrown track. (At this point you could take another lovely diversion, by turning left and continuing along the track to where the valley opens out, and then returning to this point; allow 1h30min return.) The main walk turns *right* here, back towards the ridge of Archaia Eleftherna. You pass through a wire gate almost immediately, and then join another track — the same one that you left earlier. Two sharp bends later you're back at the point where you took the path leading to the bridge.

Picnic 31: Byzantine tower at Eleftherna

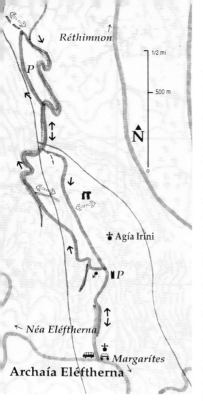

Retrace your footsteps until you get to the ancient path mentioned earlier (now on your left) and turn onto it. Almost immediately you'll see a steep path forking right: ignore it. (At this point the ridge of Archaia Eleftherna is rising on your right, and there are several ways up to it, some better than others.) The path you want is the *next* sharp turning to the right just a bit further on. Climbing many steps, ignore a small path off to the right five minutes up. Then take a very steep path curving up to the left; it squeezes its way between two large bushes, to emerge on the spine of the ridge. Head up right, through terraces, back towards the tower following the western slope of the ridge. Ignore a fork going downhill to the right; a minute later you reach a small plateau (**1h30min**). The path keeps to the western edge of the ridge, but archaeological buffs may wish to explore the fenced excavation site ahead.* The main walk continues on the path for another 10 minutes or so, until you come back to the ancient cisterns. From here retrace your footsteps up the cobblestone path, past the Byzantine tower and back to the Acropolis Taverna (**1h45min**).

*If you wish to explore the ancient site properly, continue on the path following the western edge of the ridge. In four minutes you'll see a small path climbing sharp left through a makeshift wire gate; follow it. This path emerges on another plateau in the centre of which is the barrel-vaulted (roofless) church of Agia Irini. Returning to the main path, a couple of minutes further on you come to the last of the little surprises on this walk: look left for another path which climbs a bank up to another plateau (only about 30m/yds wide). Cross to the far (eastern) side of it to where you will find a path leading down to a kind of ledge. A few paces further on you will come to the entrance of an ancient tunnel cut out of the rock. (A torch would come in handy here.) The entrance looks quite small, but the tunnel is surprisingly large once you are inside it. It was apparently used in ancient times to carry water from the cistern to the dwellings on the eastern slope of the ridge.

Bus times are *not* written in stone; seasonal changes are made in mid-May and mid-September. *The timetables given here are 'summer' timetables* — valid for the height of the season. Buses are likely to be less frequent in spring and autumn. Be sure to collect an up-to-date timetable from the bus station. Enquire about early-morning buses in particular if you think there is one (ie, if we have stated that there is one) because there's a chance they'll think you wouldn't dream of getting up at the crack of dawn when you're on holiday! Note, too, that there are other buses running from the resorts: ask for local timetables when you arrive. **Express buses** are unlikely to stop at intermediate destinations. See Index to locate quickly the timetable number for each destination; see pages 8-9 for bus stations.

Buses from Hania

1 Hania–Rethimnon; daily; journey 1h (continues to Iraklion; see Timetable 2 below)
Departures from Hania: 05.30, 06.30, 07.30, 08.00, 08.30, 09.00, 09.30, 10.00, 10.30, 11.00, 11.30, 12.00, 12.30, 13.00, 13.30, 14.00, 14.30, 15.00, 15.30, 16.00, 16.30, 17.00, 17.30, 18.30, 19.30, 20.30. *Express: 08.45, 09.15, 11.15*
Departures from Rethimnon: 06.15, 07.00, 07.30, 08.30, 09.00, 09.30, 10.00, 10.30, 11.00, 11.30, 12.00, 12.30, 13.00, 13.30, 14.00, 14.30, 15.00, 15.30, 16.00, 16.30, 17.00, 17.30, 18.00, 18.30, 19.00, 19.30, 20.00, 20.30, 21.00, 22.00. *Express: 12.45, 13.45, 15.45*

2 Hania–Iraklion (via Rethimnon); daily; journey 2h
Departures from Hania: as Timetable 1 above
Departures from Iraklion: 05.30, 06.30, 07.30, 08.00, 08.30, 09.00, 09.30, 10.00, 10.30, 11.00, 11.30, 12.00, 12.30, 13.00, 13.30, 14.00, 14.30, 15.00, 15.30, 16.00, 16.30, 17.00, 17.30, 18.00, 18.30, 19.00, 19.30, 20.00, 20.30. *Express: 11.15, 12,15, 14.15*

3 Hania–Omalos; daily; journey about 45min
Departures from Hania: 06.15, 07.30, 08.30, 10.30
Departures from Omalos: 07.30, 08.45, 09.45, 17.45

4 Hania–Hora Sfakion; daily; journey about 2h
Departures from Hania: 08.30, 11.00, 14.00
Departures from Hora Sfakion: 07.00, 11.00, 16.30, 18.30

5 Hania–Paleohora; daily; journey 2h
Departures from Hania: 08.30, 10.30, 12.00, 14.30, 17.00
Departures from Paleohora: 07.00, 12.00, 13.30, 15.30, 18.00

6 Hania–Sougia; daily; journey 1h30min
Departures from Hania: 08.30, 13.30
Departures from Sougia: 07.00, 17.00

7 Hania–Kolimbari; daily; journey 30min
Departures from Hania: 06.00, 07.15, 08.00, 08.30, 08.45, 09.15, 09.30, 10.00, 10.30, 11.00, 11.30, 12.00, 12.30, 13.00, 13.30, 14.00, 14.30, 15.00, 15.30, 16.30, 17.30, 18.00, 18.30, 19.30, 20.00, 20.30, 21.00, 21.30, 22.00, 22.30
Departures from Kolimbari: 05.20, 06.30, 07.20, 07.45, 08.00, 08.20, 08.50, 09.00, 09.20, 09.50, 10.00, 10.10, 10.40, 10.50, 11.10, 11.30, 11.40, 11.50, 12.10, 12.40, 13.00, 13.10, 14.10, 14.20, 14.40, 15.00, 15.40, 15.50, 16.10, 16.40, 17.00, 17.10, 17.50, 18.10, 18.30, 19.30, 20.00, 20.10, 20.40, 21.10, 21.40, 22.10

8 Hania–Kastelli-Kissamou; daily; journey 45min
Departures from Hania: 06.00, 07.15, 08.30, 09.00, 10.00, 11.00, 12.00, 13.00, 14.00, 15.30, 16.30, 17.30, 18.30, 19.30, 20.30
Departures from Kastelli: 05.00, 06.00, 07.00, 07.30, 08.00, 08.30, 09.30, 10.30, 11.00, 12.30, 14.00, 15.30, 16.30, 17.30, 18.30, 19.30

9 Hania–Kato Stalos–Agia Marina–Platanias–Maleme; daily
Departures from Hania: 08.15 and every 15min until 11.00; 11.30 and every 30min until 16.00; 16.15 and every 15min until 19.30; 20.00 and every 30min until 23.00
Departures from Maleme Beach Hotel: 08.15 and every 15min until 11.00; 11.30 and every 30min until 16.00; 16.15 and every 15min until 19.30; 19.45 and every 30min until 22.45

10 Hania–Elafonisi (and Moni Chrisoskalitisas); daily; journey 1h15min
Departures from Hania: 08.00
Departures from Elafonisi: 16.00

11 Hania–Plakias (via Rethimnon); daily; journey 1h45min
Departures from Hania: 06.30, 07.30, 08.00, 10.00, 12.30, 14.30, 16.00
Departures from Plakias: 07.00, 09.15, 09.30, 11.05, 13.05, 15.00, 17.30, 19.00

Buses from Rethimnon

12 Rethimnon–Hania; daily; journey 1h
Departures from Rethimnon: See Timetable 1
Departures from Hania: See Timetable 1

13 Rethimnon–Iraklion; daily; journey 1h30min
Departures from Rethimnon: 06.30, 07.30, 07.45, 08.30, 08.45, 09.15, 09.45, 10.15, 10.45, 11.15, 11.45, 12.15, 12.45, 13.15, 13.45, 14.00, 14.15, 14.45, 15.15, 15.45, 16.15, 16.45, 17.15, 17.45, 18.15, 18.45, 19.45, 20.45, 21.45. ***Express: 09.45, 10.15, 12.15***
Departures from Iraklion: See Timetable 2

14 Rethimnon–Preveli; daily *in summer only;* journey 40min
Departures from Rethimnon: 09.30, 11.30, 16.00, 17.30
Departures from Preveli: 10.35, 12.35, 17.05, 18.35

15 Rethimnon–Asomatos–Plakias; daily; journey 40min
Departures from Rethimnon: 06.15, 08.00, 09.30, 11.30, 14.15, 16.00
Departures from Plakias: as Timetable 11 above

16 Rethimnon–Hora Sfakion; daily; journey 1h30min
Departures from Rethimnon: 08.00, 14.15 (not Sat, Sun)
Departures from Hora Sfakion: 11.00 (not Sat, Sun), 17.30

17 Rethimnon–Omalos; daily; journey 2h30min
Departures from Rethimnon: 06.15, 07.00
Departures from Omalos: via Hania; see Timetable 3 above

18 Rethimnon–Eleftherna; daily; journey 1h
Departures from Rethimnon: 06.15, 10.30, 12.45
Departures from Eleftherna: 07.00, 11.05, 16.00

19 Rethimnon–Timbaki–Mires (for Kamares); Mon-Fri; journey 1h30min-2h
Departure from Rethimnon: 07.00
Departure from Kamares: 13.50

Buses from Kastelli-Kissamou (see also Timetable 8 above)

20 Kastelli–Hania–Omalos; daily; journey 3h
Departures from Kastelli: 05.00, 06.00, 07.00, 14.00
Departures from Omalos: via Hania; see Timetable 3 above

21 Kastelli–Hania–Hora Sfakion; daily; journey 3h45min
Departures from Kastelli: via Hania; see Timetables 4 and 8
Departures from Hora Sfakion: 17.30

Index

Geographical names comprise the only entries in this Index. For other entries, see Contents, page 3. A page number in *italic type* indicates a map reference; a page number in **bold type** indicates a photograph. Both of these may be in addition to a text reference on the same page. Bus timetables are on pages 133-134.

135